D0779498
crochet
TAXIDERMY
30 Quirky Animal Projects,
from Mouse to Moose
TAYLOR HART
Storey Publishing
SOMERSET CO. LIBRARY
BRIDGEWATER, N.J. 08807

To my loving husband, Matt,
who has stood by me and helped guide me
through all my hopes and dreams

The mission of Storey Publishing is to serve our customers by publishing practical information that encourages personal independence in harmony with the environment.

Edited by Gwen Steege and Jessica Miller-Smith
Art direction and book design by Alethea Morrison
Text production by Jennifer Jepson Smith
Indexed by Valerie Shrader

Cover and interior photography by Mars Vilaubi
Illustrations on pages 10–11, 30–31, 43–44, 55–56, and 70–71 by © Meg Hunt
How-to illustrations by Brigita Fuhrmann

Storey books are available for special premium and promotional uses and for customized editions. For further information, please call 1-800-793-9396.

Storey Publishing
210 MASS MoCA Way
North Adams, MA 01247
www.storey.com

Printed in China by R.R. Donnelley
10 9 8 7 6 5 4 3 2 1

LIBRARY OF CONGRESS CATALOGING-IN-PUBLICATION DATA
Names: Hart, Taylor, author.
Title: Crochet taxidermy : 30 quirky animal projects, from mouse to moose / Taylor Hart.
Description: North Adams, MA : Storey Publishing, [2016] | Includes index.
Identifiers: LCCN 2016008768 (print) | LCCN 2016020731 (ebook) | ISBN 9781612127361 (pbk. : alk. paper) | ISBN 9781612127378 (Ebook)
Subjects: LCSH: Soft toys. | Crocheting—Patterns.
Classification: LCC TT174.3 .H425 2016 (print) | LCC TT174.3 (ebook) | DDC 745.592/4—dc23
LC record available at https://lccn.loc.gov/2016008768

CONTENTS

Asia
Indian
Ocean

RAISING CHICKENS
CHICKEN
FARM ANATOMY
Milk

HELLO THERE!

When my husband and I moved from Columbus, Ohio, to Austin, Texas, in 2008, it was in hopes of starting over again, fresh. Like many places across the country at the time, businesses in Ohio were shutting down and unemployment was on the rise. As was true for many college graduates, I couldn't find a job in my field of photography, so I was working for a large insurance company. The BFA I had worked so hard for wasn't being put to good use in my beige cubicle. So we decided that it was time for us to make a big change in our lives. My husband sent out résumés, and to our great delight, he landed a job at his first interview, a position in Austin. We packed up what belongings we could fit into a tiny U-Haul and took off two weeks later with our puppy, Lucy, on our new adventure.

It was here in Austin that I taught myself to crochet. After our move, I began my own job hunt and managed to trade my beige cubicle in Ohio for a gray one at a call center in Texas. In between calls, I picked up a beginner's crochet book and instantly fell in love with my newfound hobby. I never thought that I'd be making a full-time career out of it nor writing this very book you're reading. In fact, it was merely something fun to do with my fellow coworkers, but it soon it became my passion.

After crocheting some small toys using the Japanese technique of amigurumi, I slowly discovered that I could make and create my own little critters. I began to design some unique, fun plushy toys and started selling them down on South Congress, the wonderful section in the heart of Austin filled with boutiques and eateries. I was delighted to find that people adored my little toys as much as I loved to create them. It was in that setting that I discovered a whole new world of "handmade." I was surrounded by people just like me: people filled with the same passion and desire to make and create. Coming from Columbus, I'd somehow missed the whole handmade boat that was sweeping much of the country. DIY was our generation's answer to our dwindling economy, as we discovered ways of hand-making quality goods by ourselves and for ourselves, without having to rely on or spend a whole lot of money at large chain stores. I had unwittingly landed in a hot spot of DIY, and I am grateful that I did.

The woodland creatures in the first section of the book are the first crocheted taxidermy heads I created, and they're near and dear to my heart.

My whole taxidermy line was, in fact, the result of a happy accident. In between making my amigurumi critters to sell, I would often make a little something for myself. I had been working on my own design for a faux fox scarf, and although I had a great base scarf, the fox head didn't look quite right after I attached it. My husband suggested that I mount the fox head on a plaque to hang on our wall. I thought the idea was incredibly, oddly adorable and rushed out to my local craft store to buy a wooden plaque. I stained the plaque, and together we figured out how to mount it and proudly hung a crocheted faux fox head in our living room for all to see.

All our friends and neighbors thought Mr. Fox was too cute and clever for me not to make and sell, so I slowly started to create more designs and patterns and introduced my woodland creatures to Austin. People were oddly struck by my little creations. They made them smile and then laugh, and the critters were a big success. I soon began selling them on Etsy and in local boutiques throughout Austin, launched my lifestyle blog *Nothing but a Pigeon*, joined forces with the local craft group Austin Craft Riot, and began showing and selling my creatures in both Texas and Ohio. Now, my part-time hobby has become my full-time reality.

I am thrilled to be able to compile the patterns and designs that have brought me so much joy to make and sell over the years and to share them with you so you can make and create them for your very own. Whether you're making them to hang in your child's nursery or creating them as a gift for a friend or family member, these patterns are easy to read and follow. Even a beginner can learn to crochet from this book. That's exactly how I learned, and I'd like to help you do it, too. I hope my book will inspire you to crochet your very own creations to hang on your wall and enjoy. There are no limitations to what you can create.

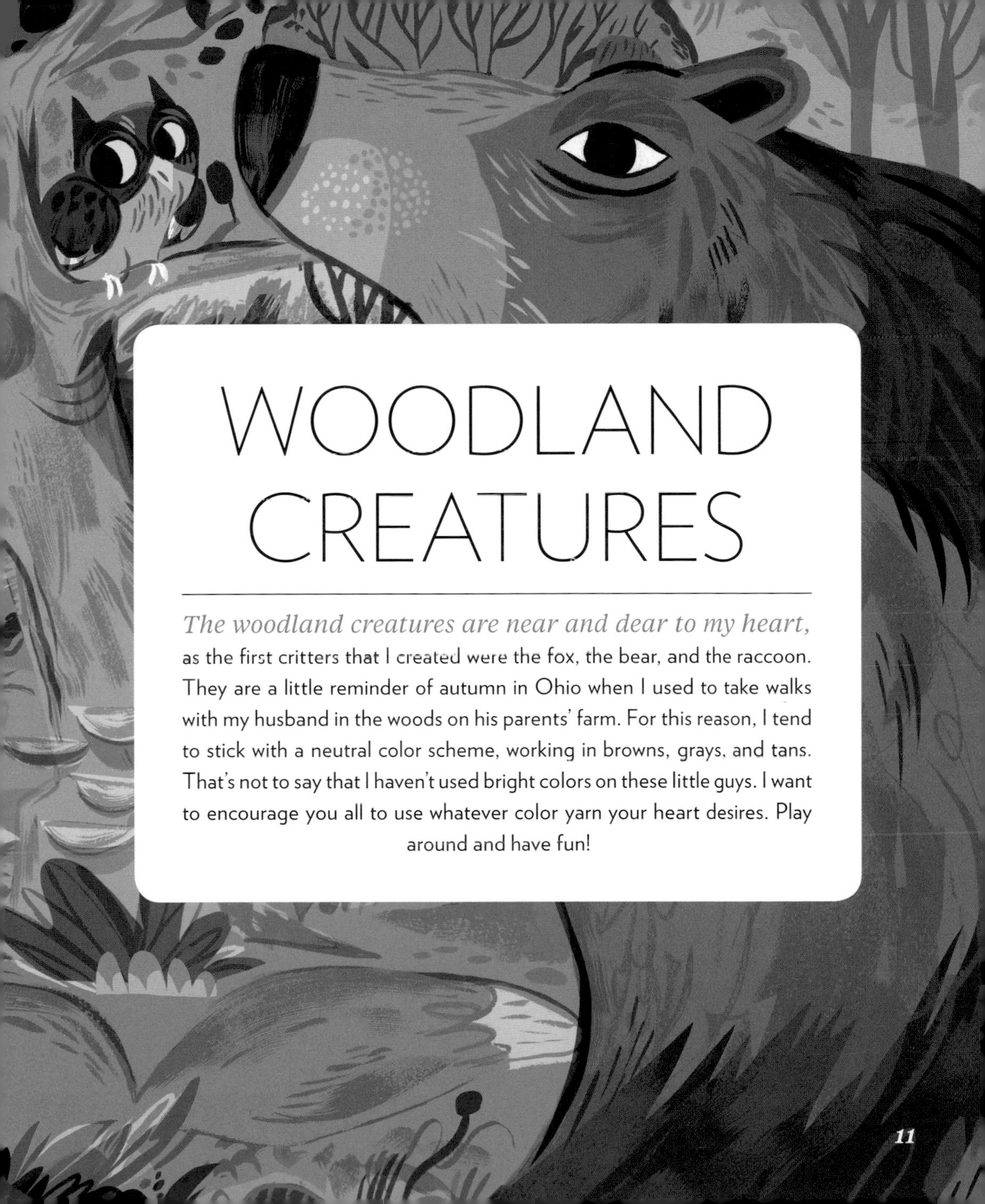

WOODLAND CREATURES

The woodland creatures are near and dear to my heart, as the first critters that I created were the fox, the bear, and the raccoon. They are a little reminder of autumn in Ohio when I used to take walks with my husband in the woods on his parents' farm. For this reason, I tend to stick with a neutral color scheme, working in browns, grays, and tans. That's not to say that I haven't used bright colors on these little guys. I want to encourage you all to use whatever color yarn your heart desires. Play around and have fun!

Shy Deer

Is it hunting season already? This little buck is lying low over here and looking all shy for good reason. He has the most adorable little two-point rack and the sleepiest of eyelids.

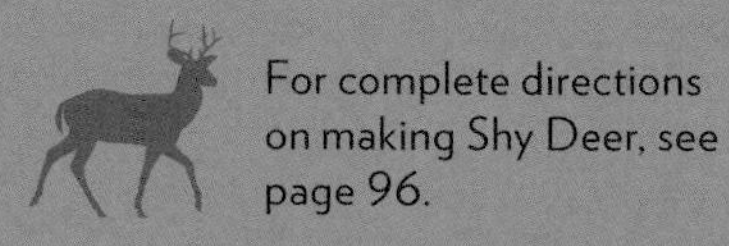

For complete directions on making Shy Deer, see page 96.

Sly Fox

This little guy with white-tipped ears is the first critter I ever created. My husband always tells me that my spirit animal is a fox, and I have to agree. There is something about this tiny creature that has always intrigued me, so maybe that's why I chose him as my first creation.

For complete directions on making Sly Fox, see page 100.

Rowdy Raccoon

Guess who's up to his ol' nighttime shenanigans again? This wee bandit is based on my little foxy pattern but has an added black band across his face, because he needs a mask — for his hijinks of course.

For complete directions on making Rowdy Raccoon, see page 103.

Monumental Moose

This gentle giant is the biggest critter in the book, but he's well worth all the hard work and dedication.

For complete directions on making Monumental Moose, see page 106.

Brown Bear

The brown bear is another favorite of mine and one of the first I made. This beady-eyed bear is a most chocolaty shade of brown, but your bear can be whatever color you'd like, from light blond to golden or plain brown, just as in nature. Have fun and experiment.

For complete directions on making Brown Bear, see page 113.

Little Stinker

Do you smell something? Oh no, it's a skunk! Be on the lookout for this cute little stinker. You can always spot a skunk by its stripes. In this tiny, whimsical pattern, I introduce specialty yarn — the fluffy, fuzzy kind that is really fun to use.

For complete directions on making Little Stinker, see page 116.

Meek Mouse

Eeeeeeek! There's a mouse in the house!! It's okay, guys — he's just a wee little crocheted mouse stuffed with fluff and not the real deal. Meek Mouse is based on my Little Stinker pattern and is a superfast, fun pattern that's easy enough for a beginner.

For complete directions on making Meek Mouse, see page 119.

Mallard Duck

With his dark green head and white-and-brown banded neck, this little duckie is no stranger to northern territory.

For complete directions on making Mallard Duck, see page 121.

Little Hooter

Hoot, hoot! Is that a barn owl I hear? With so many different species of owls to consider, these little hooded hooters could be crocheted in a variety of colors, from their hoods right down to their pointy little beaks.

For complete directions on making Little Hooter, see page 123.

FARM FRIENDS

Come hang out down on the farm with me and all my crochet buddies. As you already know, I grew up in Ohio where there is farmland as far as the eye can see. I'm a city gal mostly, but my husband grew up raising cattle and tending to the land. These little guys are an ode to him and all the crazy farm stories he has from growing up in the Midwest.

Pinky Pig

What's farm life without cute little piglets tromping around? This little oinker is the softest shade of pink right down to its little piggy nostrils and ears.

For complete directions on making Pinky Pig, see page 127.

Baaaad Sheep

This soft, cuddly little sheep has just been sheared, but you could always make yours extra fuzzy by adding specialty yarn as an option to his white coat.

For complete directions on making Baaaad Sheep, see page 130.

How Now, Brown Cow

This brown cow has been grazing all day out in the fields with his other colorful cow friends. Why, there is an orange Longhorn, a black Angus, and a light beige Guernsey. Crochet any type of cow you can think of by just changing the color of the nose and head, and giving it horns or not!

For complete directions on making How Now, Brown Cow, see page 133.

Dairy Cow

Ice cream, anyone? This black-and-white dairy cow is ready to be milked. Based on my How Now, Brown Cow pattern, this little milk shake comes with a few added spots but without horns.

For complete directions on making Dairy Cow, see page 137.

Farm Duck

Picture this all-yellow, orange-billed farm duck waddling near the pond. Farm ducks come in many other shades, so make your farm duckie your own by personalizing its colors.

For complete directions on making Farm Duck, see page 141.

A Hen and a Rooster

These guys are an ode to the little feathered friends that run around in our backyard. My husband and I love to go outside and watch our chickens scamper and frolic around when we feed them. It's been a true joy watching them grow from wee little chicks to beautiful hens.

For complete directions on making A Hen and a Rooster, see page 143.

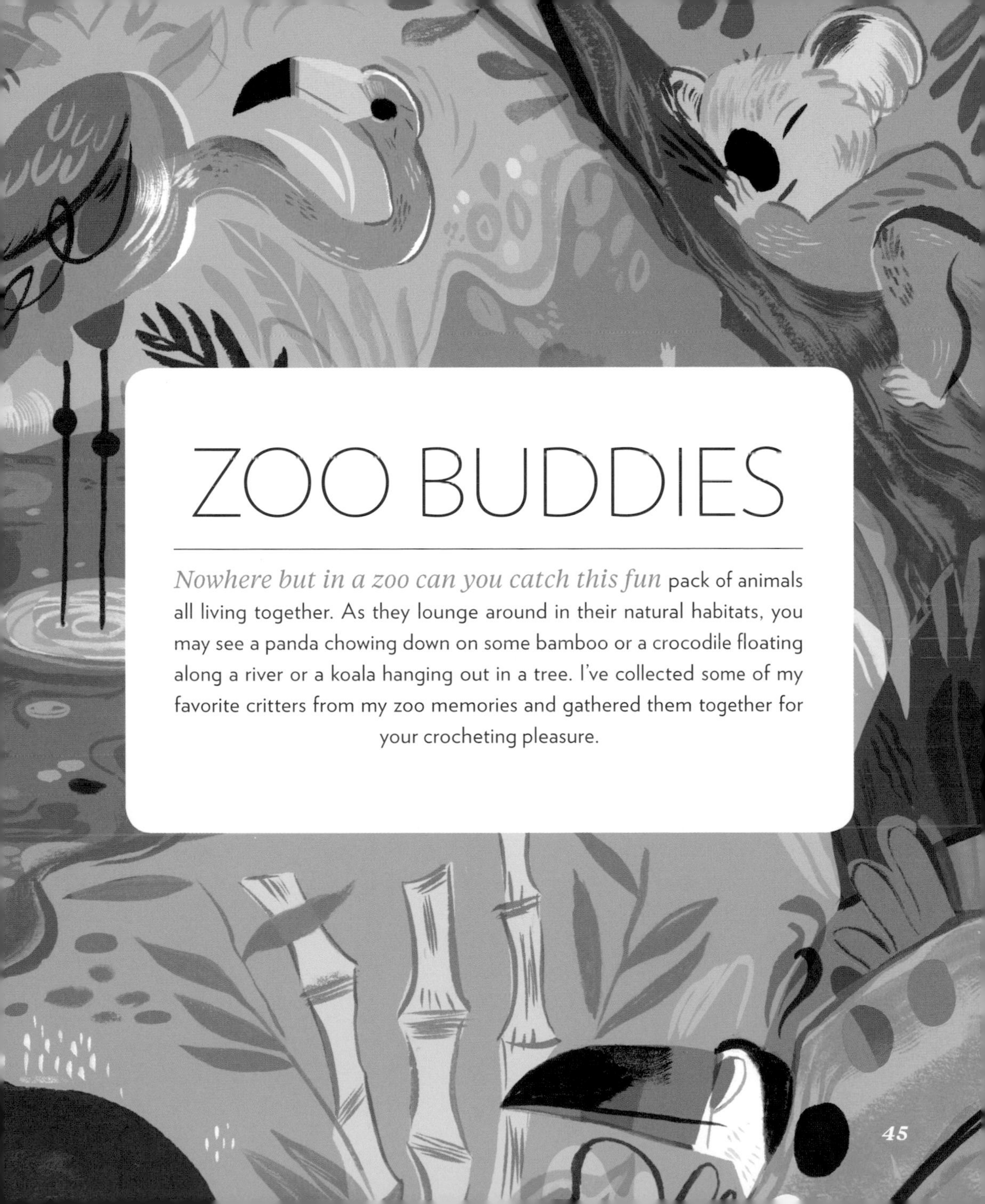

ZOO BUDDIES

Nowhere but in a zoo can you catch this fun pack of animals all living together. As they lounge around in their natural habitats, you may see a panda chowing down on some bamboo or a crocodile floating along a river or a koala hanging out in a tree. I've collected some of my favorite critters from my zoo memories and gathered them together for your crocheting pleasure.

Cranky Croc

Don't stick your arms anywhere near the crocodile's space! Cranky crocs may be hungry for dinner and bite on just about anything!

For complete directions on making Cranky Croc, see page 146.

Flora Flamingo

Flora has been busy eating many shrimp, which make her and her flamingo friends turn a very delicate shade of pink. You can make your flamingo as pink your heart desires. The more shrimp flamingos eat, the pinker they get!

For complete directions on making Flora Flamingo, see page 150.

Krazy Koala

The fuzzy, lovable koala bear is such a lazybones, sleeping in a tree all day long and eating leaves. This is a really fun pattern that uses specialty yarn for the ears. This one is wide awake, but I sometimes like to add the "sleepy eye" effect to my koalas.

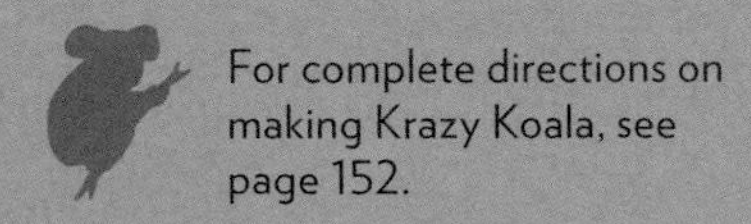

For complete directions on making Krazy Koala, see page 152.

Panda Bear

This shy, cuddly panda lives high in dense bamboo forests of China and spends about 12 hours a day eating bamboo, which is 99 percent of his diet. Let's give this meek panda bear some privacy while he eats his fill.

For complete directions on making Panda Bear, see page 156.

Timid Toucan

Toucan feels right at home in his rain-forest-themed habitat. With his beautiful beak and fun tuft of feathers that flutters around in the breeze, he is full of vibrant colors. You can use whatever bold and brilliant colors you choose for his beak.

For complete directions on making Timid Toucan, see page 160.

SAFARI FRIENDS

Take out those binoculars and hold on tight because we're going on a safari! Can you spot the herd of elephants over there? Or how 'bout that hippo swimming around in the water, wiggling his little hippo ears? And did you see that lion with his majestic mane? All these safari friends have unique qualities, from the giraffe's ossicones right down to the zebra's black and white stripes.

Ellie the Elephant

What cute little tusks you have, Ellie! This adorable elephant would be lovely in many different shades of color. Whether you choose gray or vibrant blue, you'll have a lovable little critter to cherish for life.

For complete directions on making Ellie the Elephant, see page 163.

Graceful Giraffe

Did you know that those little nubs on top of a giraffe's head are actually bone and are called *ossicones*? This graceful giraffe's nubs are looking snazzy and are stuffed with fluff, making her quite unique.

For complete directions on making Graceful Giraffe, see page 167.

Hipster Hippo

I love the adorable duo of the Hipster Hippo and the critter that follows, the Renegade Rhino. Based on the same pattern, they make quite the pair.

For complete directions on making Hipster Hippo, see page 171.

Renegade Rhino

Whereas the Hipster Hippo in the preceding pattern displayed her pearly whites, this rhino shows off his horns. They'd make a great pair hanging on anyone's wall, wouldn't you say?

For complete directions on making Renegade Rhino, see page 175.

Lazy Lion

This sleepy lion is off duty. When he's not being king of the jungle, he's taking a little catnap under a shady tree. Don't let his soft, fluffy mane and sleepy eyes fool you — he is one mighty lion!

For complete directions on making Lazy Lion, see page 179.

Zippy Zebra

Did you know that zebras' stripes are unique to each individual animal? There's no domesticating this fast-running horsey, but his mohawk is pretty cool, huh?

For complete directions on making Zippy Zebra, see page 182.

UNDER-THE-SEA CREATURES

This last section features some of my favorite creatures to crochet. I've always been attracted to the sea and everything that lives in it. I'm thrilled to share my two favorite patterns of all time with you: the little Cute Cuttlefish and the Jiggly Jellyfish. For me, these are the most delightful critters to crochet, and they bring a smile to my face every time I work on one. Adding to the menagerie, the Colossal Squid makes an appearance, as well as my newest creation, Sleepy Octopus.

Colossal Squid

This big boy is straight out of a science-fiction novel, with his long tentacles and big bobbly eyes. He looks great crocheted in the most vibrant of colors.

For complete directions on making Colossal Squid, see page 186.

Cute Cuttlefish

This cute little guy is fun and quick to make. I love the cuttlefish's baby tentacles; he looks super in all shades of blue or green.

For complete directions on making Cute Cuttlefish, see page 190.

Sleepy Octopus

This octopus is busy dreaming about all the tiny crabs he's going to eat for his next meal. This tubby and very sleepy guy looks great in all shades of blue.

For complete directions on making Sleepy Octopus, see page 193.

Jiggly Jellyfish

My favorite critter to make has to be the Jiggly Jellyfish. Not only is he freaking adorable, but I just love stitching in his little V-shaped smile and seeing his face come to life.

For complete directions on making Jiggly Jellyfish, see page 196.

STARTING WITH THE BASICS

You'll find a lot of different crochet techniques out there in the world. If you know the basics, then feel free to jump right in and start your first project. If you are a beginner, don't fret. I cover all the stitches in the appendix, so you can flip back and forth as needed. In this chapter, I cover the main crochet techniques that I've found to be the most useful and incorporate in all my patterns. I also give a bit of advice about yarns, as well as important add-ons, like plastic safety eyes and fiberfill. Finally, I explain how to prep your plaques and mount your little critters.

ALL ABOUT THE YARN

For most of the critter's heads and bodies, you can use any worsted-weight yarn. Look for the symbol (4) on the yarn band. I use mostly acrylic yarns, but if you prefer to work in nothing but natural fibers, they crochet up beautifully as well. The important thing is to choose a crochet hook size that combines with your yarn to create a dense fabric that completely covers the fiberfill. When I use acrylic yarn (worsted-weight size 4), I find that a size US F/5 (3.75 mm) hook works well, but when I use worsted wool (also size 4), I get better coverage with the next hook size smaller, US E/4 (3.5 mm). The final measurements of your critter may differ from mine due to your choice of yarn and hook and/or your crochet technique.

For me, other requirements are that the yarn is soft and easily slides through my fingers. It's exciting to shop for fun colors that will give just the right amount of believability to each of your taxidermy critters. You'll find suggestions with each of the patterns, but feel free to experiment with your own color choices.

A few of the projects, such as Little Skunk, Lazy Lion, and Krazy Koala, feature specialty yarns for details like the lion's mane and the koala's fuzzy-tipped ears. For Cranky Croc's teeth, you'll need a lighter-weight yarn, perhaps a DK (3), and a smaller hook (US E/4, 3.5 mm) as well. You'll find advice about all of this with the individual patterns. (For more about working with specialty yarns, see Here Comes the Fuzz on page 88.)

TAXIDERMY CRITTER TECHNIQUES

These are my tried-and-true techniques that I use again and again in all my patterns. See page 202 for a list of supplies.

Using a split ring marker

Changing the yarn color (A)

Changing the yarn color (B)

CROCHETING IN THE ROUND

I use this technique in every one of my patterns. Crocheting in the round is essentially working a continuous spiral of single crochet, building on top of each preceding round. Keep track by marking the end of one round and the beginning of the next with a split-ring stitch marker that you can move along as you work. This is especially important when you are making the increases and decreases that form the little guy's shape.

CHANGING THE YARN COLOR

A few patterns require you to change yarn colors while crocheting. To do this, begin the last single crochet in the old color (A). When you have 2 loops on your hook, yarnover with the new color, and draw the new yarn through both loops (B). Be sure to weave both the ending and beginning tails into the wrong side of the fabric for several stitches to neaten and secure the join (for illustration, see page 84). You can use this same technique if you run out of yarn and need to start a new yarn, even of the same color.

WHIPSTITCHING TO JOIN PIECES

I use this technique to join two pieces of crochet work, such as the koala bear's ears (page 153). Position the pieces to be joined with wrong sides facing each other. Thread a yarn needle with a length of matching yarn. Insert the needle through both pieces, then take the yarn over the edge and insert the needle into the next crochet stitch on the same side as your first stitch. Continue in this way until you come to the last available single crochet stitch. Pass the yarn through the last stitch to fasten off, then weave in the tail on the wrong side.

Whipstitching to join pieces

FASTENING OFF

Sometimes called finishing off, this is simply how you end a row or round of crochet and secure your yarn. Slipstitch into the nearest available stitch or space (A) (see also Slipstitch, page 201). Cut the yarn, leaving a 6-inch tail, and draw the tail through the loop on the hook to fasten off (B). Thread the tail into a yarn needle and weave it in on the wrong side of the crochet fabric. In some cases, you'll need to leave a 12-inch-long tail (or longer), which you'll be instructed to leave unwoven and use later in the pattern to sew pieces together. Advice about this is given in each project.

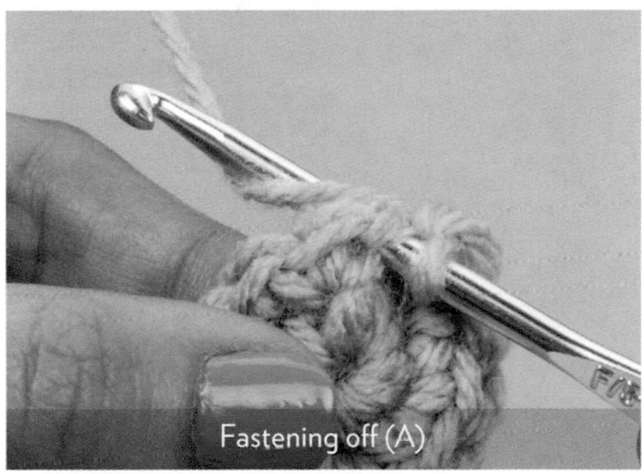

Fastening off (A)

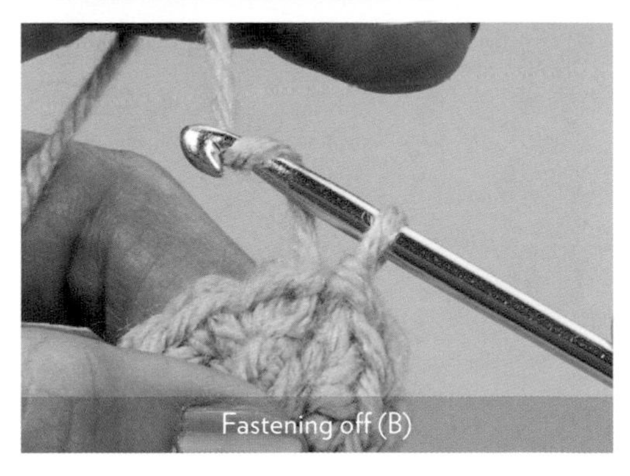

Fastening off (B)

Weaving in loose ends

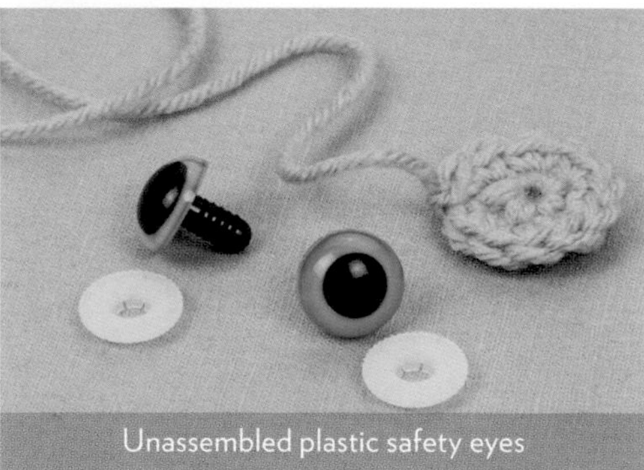
Unassembled plastic safety eyes

Plastic Eye Warning

When you sew on the crocheted roundie (see facing page), be sure the safety eye is already secured through both the roundie and the head fabric with the plastic backing (washer) clicked into place. These eyes and noses rarely come out, but they can be a choking hazard to little ones, so do not use them where kiddos under the age of three will be able to get at them, and always make sure they are secure.

WEAVING IN LOOSE ENDS

You don't want your critter's head looking all sloppy, so you've got to weave in all those loose ends to keep it looking fresh. This is done with a yarn needle. Simply thread your tail of yarn through the needle, and then weave it in and out on the wrong side of the fabric several times until it looks neat and is secure. Trim any extra tail. Now, that looks good!

CREATING FACES

Adding eyes and noses, as well as appendages like ears, horns, and teeth, requires some patience and practice. When I first started sewing appendages onto my critters years ago, they looked pretty strange. Now, I'm a pro at it. When you're stitching the various pieces in place, it's important to use a good yarn needle and to keep your yarn smooth: try to maintain yarn tension that's not too tight or too loose, and don't mess around so much with the yarn that it starts to fray.

Each pattern specifies when to attach the eyes and noses, as well as which pieces are needed. In most cases, I sew eyes and/or eye roundies (and noses and/or nose roundies) in place before completing the critter, when the area behind these items is already partially stuffed with fiberfill. If I use plastic eyes or noses, I use only what are called "safety or craft eyes" (and noses) for all my critters. (See Plastic Eye Warning at left for advice about age restrictions for the use of these items.) Both safety eyes and safety noses come in a variety of sizes and shapes, many of which are intended for particular creatures, such as dogs, cats, teddy bears, and so on. These items have two pieces: the eye (or nose) itself, which is backed with a shaft, and a separate washer that you click onto the shaft to secure it.

Here's how I construct the eyes on most of my critters. As backing, I crochet a small circle that I call a "roundie." To assemble the plastic eyes and roundies, I insert the shaft of the commerical plastic eye through the roundie and into the head fabric, and then I lock the eye in place by clicking the washer onto the shaft coming through at the back of the fabric (A). To sew the edge of the roundies down, I thread a yarn needle with the long tail I left when I slipped the last stitch of the roundie. Using small backstitches, I insert the needle through each crochet stitch close to the roundie's edge, and pull the yarn taut on the wrong side of the fabric as I work each stitch all the way around (B).

Although I use plastic safety noses for many of my critters, including the fox, deer, and bears, others don't require plastic safety noses. The cow, giraffe, and zebra, for example, feature simple roundies as nostrils. The safety noses are assembled and secured following the same process as for eyes.

Assembling a safety eye and eye roundie (A)

Assembling a safety eye and eye roundie (B)

A VARIETY OF EARS

The ears for the raccoon, fox, and bear are crocheted as tubes that are then flattened in order to sew the bottom edges closed. All others are crocheted as flat disks, some of which are folded and shaped to create the characteristic look of the animal; a few (koala and lion, for instance) are created by sewing two flat disks together. The pattern for the flat ears is similar to that for roundies, but the ears are different diameters, depending on the animal.

For the folded style, when you have completed the crocheting and fastened off the last stitch of the disk, fold the ear in half with wrong sides together and the yarn tail in the middle of the open edge. Thread the tail through a yarn needle and whipstitch the edges together from the center of the opening to the fold, leaving the other half of the ear open. Fasten off the last stitch and draw the tail through, leaving it long so that you can use it later to stitch the ear to the head.

Tube ear

Two-piece flat disk ear

Folded disk ear

SLEEPY-EYE TECHNIQUE

I use this technique for several of my critters: the Shy Deer, Lazy Lion, and Sleepy Octopus. It's an easy way of creating an eyelid after the eyes are fastened in place, and I love the sleepy look it makes. Thread a yarn needle with yarn the same color as the head. Starting on the wrong side of the fabric, draw the needle up through the front as close as possible to the eye, pass the yarn over the eye to the opposite edge, and then to the back. Repeat this pass four or five times until you get the look you're trying to achieve. Fasten off on the wrong side and weave in the yarn tail.

Sleepy-eye technique

MAKING A "BUTTONHOLE"

A few of my patterns (the Under-the-Sea Creatures starting on page 186, for instance) call for crocheting a small hole, or "buttonhole," to allow the dowel to peek through the fabric where the little guy will be mounted on the plaque. To create this buttonhole, crochet to the point indicated in the pattern where you need to create the hole. Instead of continuing single crochet stitches, skip 2 or 3 stitches (A), as indicated by the pattern, then make the same number of chains as the skipped stitches (B). When you come to the chains in the following row or round, single chain 2 or 3 stitches (per pattern) in the space made by the chain (ch-space) to bring you back to the original number of stitches in the row or round.

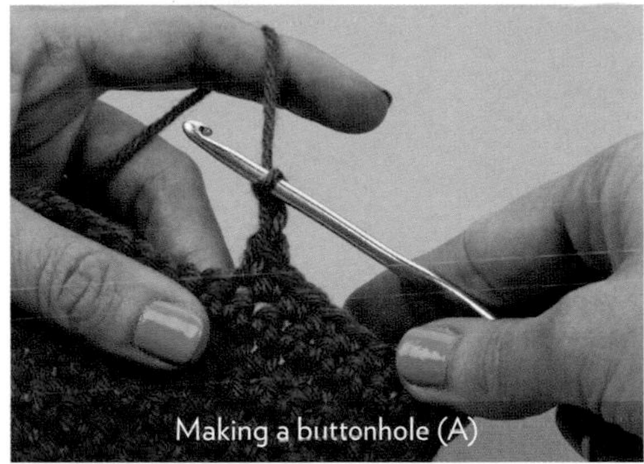
Making a buttonhole (A)

Making a buttonhole (B)

HERE COMES THE FUZZ

I like to use specialty yarn, such as eyelash yarn or faux fur yarn, for some of my critters. You can see it in Lazy Lion's mane, Krazy Koala's fuzzy ears, and the Little Skunk's stripe. This technique requires a little bit of primping or fluffing during and after the process. I typically use a smaller hook as well to help keep a tight grip on my yarn. The fuzz is very thin and super slippery, and sometimes it's hard to see where you're actually crocheting. Although specialty yarn is labeled bulky, I find it easier to use a smaller hook, such as a US D/3 (3.25 mm) or E/4 (3.5 mm), to help aid my grip when pulling the thin yarn through the stitches.

Work in your specialty yarn a single crochet stitch at a time (A), hand fluffing along the way (B). It's helpful to keep your critter's head in your lap so that you can hold it with one hand and fluff up the fuzz with the other. Most craft stores sell special brushes for this purpose, but I prefer to use my hands.

Adding the lion's mane (A)

Adding the lion's mane (B)

STUFF ABOUT FIBERFILL

I use my hands or, occasionally, my crochet hook, to push and pull the polyester fiberfill into place so that the critter is firm. In the long run, I find it easiest to stuff my critter's heads as I crochet, and you'll find my suggestions about when to begin stuffing in the instructions for each project. There's really not just a single way to do it, however, so use whatever technique you find works best for you.

INSERTING THE DOWEL

When you're finishing up the crochet, one of the last steps is to insert the predrilled dowel into the

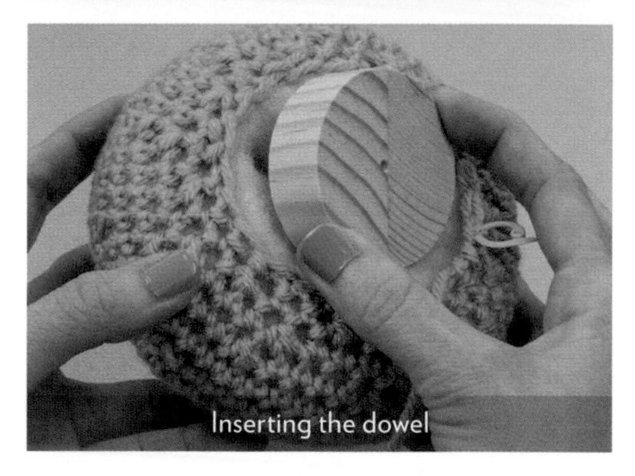
Inserting the dowel

hole and then completely close the fabric around it. (For instructions on how to prepare the dowel rods, see Cutting Your Dowel Rods, page 91.) When you insert the dowel, make sure to position it so that the screw hole is facing out, peeking through the little hole you created. It is also important to ensure that the end of the dowel is flush with the back of the critter's head. This is so that you won't run into problems centering the head when you screw the critter to the plaque. You may need to add more fiberfill around the dowel after inserting it into the opening. You'll find a reminder of this step with each pattern along with instructions for closing the hole.

Closing up around the dowel

MOUNTING YOUR CRITTER'S HEAD

Once your head is complete, you're ready for the final step in creating your very own taxidermy critter: preparing your plaque and mounting your critter on it. (See page 202 for supply list.)

Before you jump right into drilling holes through your plaque and staining it, you may want to set up an area with a worktable, some scrap wood, and a vise or clamp to hold the scrap piece of wood in place. I have a designated area where I do all my precutting and predrilling. The scrap piece of wood has saved my furniture and worktable many times.

Once you have your space set up, gather your tools and supplies: the plaque, fine-grained sandpaper or sandblock, stain and foam craft brushes, 1⅝-inch Grip-Rite drywall screws, and both a Phillips-head bit and a 7/64 wood drill with a countersink bit. (You need only one screw for each head.) It's very important that your drill bit matches the size and type of your drywall screws, because if it doesn't, you may have some issues getting your critter's head screwed on correctly.

If you're using a cordless (battery operated) drill, make sure it's all charged up and ready to go. You may also want to supply yourself with a drop cloth, smock or apron, and old clean T-shirts to protect you and your surroundings from spills.

To mount the head on the plaque, you need either a 1¼- or 2-inch diameter dowel rod and a saw to cut it. You'll also need a hammer and picture hanger to attach your taxidermy critter on the wall. (You'll find specifications for the dowel sizes required along with the list of other supplies and materials needed with each pattern.)

PREPPING YOUR PLAQUES

I always like to stain my plaques, as well as precut and predrill my dowel rods, before I jump into crocheting my critters. For one thing, drying time can take a few days based on weather. Also, you'll be anxious to mount your critter's head as soon as you finish it, and it will be anticlimactic if you can't. Regardless of what you decide to do first, here's how to proceed, along with a few tips and tricks that I have learned along the way.

Before staining your plaque, remove any stickers that are on it. This sometimes takes a little finesse and patience. Even if the stickers are on the back only, I peel them off so that I can stain the back as well as the front, because I think they just look nicer and more professional that way. If you're not concerned about staining the back of your plaque, you can skip this step. It's totally your call. You may also notice that your plaque needs to be sanded a tad as well. I like to use a fine-grain sandpaper or sandblock for this step.

The Spray Paint Option

If you decide to use spray paint, I recommend using a matte rather than a glossy finish. Matte finishes tend to be less reflective, whereas I feel that a glossy one can distract from the critter itself. Also, a matte finish doesn't show the defects in the wood as much, which can be a big deal.

After all the rough edges are smoothed out, make sure you wipe the surface thoroughly with a cloth towel or old cotton T-shirt to get rid of any debris on the plaque before you stain it.

I use the same color and type of stain for all of my plaques so that they look consistent. If you are planning on mounting and hanging a group of critters together on a wall, you may want to take this into account. I have tried many different types of stain, but my favorite brand and shade is Minwax's

Staining the plaque

English Chestnut 233. I've also used white spray paint, and it looked amazing. (See The Spray Paint Option on the facing page.)

I have a designated area where I stain my plaques, and I always use a drop cloth and wear a smock; I've found stain splatters in the weirdest places. I prefer to use foam craft brushes rather than regular paintbrushes, as I can discard a foam brush after a few uses, and no messy clean up is required. Make sure you shake your can of stain thoroughly before opening the lid. Whether you use stain or spray paint, make sure you are working in a well-ventilated area.

I begin by staining all the sides and corners of my plaque, as the wood absorbs more of the stain in those areas. It's good practice to use less stain, rather than dip your whole brush in the can and slap it on. Feel free to practice on a scrap piece of wood first. You can always wipe off any excess stain with an old cotton T-shirt, if necessary. After covering the sides and corners, I then work on the front of the plaque. I try to use even strokes and go in the same direction as the grain. When you are finished, let the stain dry. This could take a few hours or up to a day, depending on the weather. If you have a fan, let it blow over the plaque for faster drying time.

Once the top is completely dry (make sure it's not tacky), flip it over and stain the back.

I like to stain a bunch of plaques at one time. I recommend doing this if you're planning on making all (or many) of the critters in the book. It's the least fun thing to do, and if you're going do it, you might as well just get them all done at once. Check each project for the size of the plaque you will need.

A Large Exception

Because the Monumental Moose is quite large, it requires a very large dowel to be mounted. For this project only, you'll need a short length of 1″ × 6″ pine board to cut your own dowel. Be sure to purchase pine: it's much softer than most other woods on the market, and it's therefore easier to cut and drill through. Use a coffee can or an old CD to trace a circle onto the wood. In a perfect world, you would use a jigsaw to cut this puppy out, but instead you can use your handy coping saw for the job. This may take some patience, but my momma always told me, "Good things come to those who wait." You may need to use a vise or a clamp to hold it in place while you cut. After it's cut, hit it up with some sandpaper or a sanding block to smooth out the rough edges. Then go ahead and predrill it as described for the other dowels.

CUTTING YOUR DOWEL RODS

The next step is to cut the dowel rods to fit the project you're making. It would be ideal to have a tablesaw or jigsaw for cutting these guys, but you can always use a good old-fashioned woodsaw, hacksaw, or coping saw. You'll be measuring and cutting pieces about 1 inch long from either a 1¼- or a 2-inch-diameter dowel rod. You can get a lot of 1-inch pieces out of one 48-inch rod! If you're using a hacksaw, this can take awhile. You may want to use a clamp or a vise to hold your rod while you saw away. Don't worry if the pieces aren't exactly 1 inch long, but do try to make sure to cut them straight across, so that the heads won't be crooked when you mount them.

Three patterns in this book are for birds with long necks. For these birds, I use the smaller 1¼-inch-diameter dowel rod, cut about 2 inches long. It's very important to cut these dowels evenly, because if you don't, the birds are likely to have super-croooked necks when you mount them.

After you cut all the pieces needed for your critters, you need to predrill them. This saves a lot of time and heartache down the road. You can position the precut dowel lengthwise in a clamp or vise to hold it steady while you use your drill or place it flat on your worktable with a piece of scrap wood underneath to protect the surface. Use the 7/64 countersink drill bit to hit each dowel right in the center, drilling all the way through from end to end.

Once I've prepared all the wood pieces as described above, I like to dust them off and store them in a ziplock bag that's easy to get into when needed.

ATTACHING THE HEAD TO THE PLAQUE

I mount the majority of my critters' heads dead center in the middle of the plaque, although a few, such as the Colossal Squid, Cute Cuttlefish, and Jiggly Jellyfish, are mounted a little bit above center. Mark the place where you want to mount your head, and using your wood drill bit, drill into the plaque from the back side through to the front. Next, switch to your Phillips-head bit, and drill the drywall screw into place from the back side through to the front.

Drilling the screw hole through the dowel

Drilling the drywall screw into the plaque

Screwing the head onto the plaque

To attach the critter's head to the plaque, hold the plaque in one hand and the critter's head in the other, and then screw the predrilled dowel you inserted at the back of the head onto the drywall screw that you drilled into the plaque. Screw the head all the way on by hand so that it's not only tight but also aligned the way you want it on the plaque. It's perfectly fine to use your Phillips-head screwdriver to tighten the screw from the back, if necessary. Don't worry about mushing the head with your hands, as you can reshape it to get it to look the way you want after it's mounted.

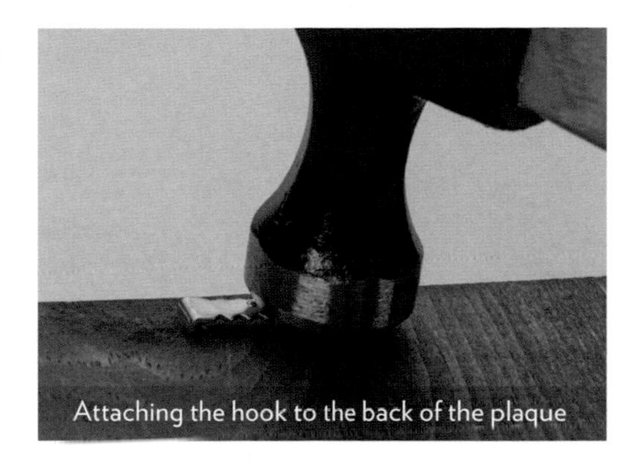
Attaching the hook to the back of the plaque

CREATING A HOOK

Once the head is screwed onto the plaque and not going anywhere, decide whether to hang it vertically or horizontally so that you can attach the wall hook. This is kind of tricky because the head makes it so you can't lay your plaque flat. To make this step possible, position the plaque so that its top lies flat on your table or workbench and the head hangs over the side. Lightly hammer the picture hook into the back side of your plaque. Sometimes the wood is so soft that you can push the picture hanger through with just your thumbs; if you use a hammer, it should take only a few gentle whacks. Voilà! Your taxidermy critter is finished, and all you have to decide is where you are going to hang it.

PROJECT DIRECTIONS

Shy Deer

Finished Measurements
- 15½″ wide × 13″ long × 5½″ deep

Hook
- US F/5 (3.75 mm) crochet hook

Yarn
- Worsted weight; 1 skein each of tan and light gray (4)

Other Supplies
- One 22 mm black plastic animal safety nose
- Two 18 mm clear plastic animal safety eyes
- Split-ring stitch marker
- Yarn needle
- Fiberfill
- Precut, predrilled dowel: 2″ diameter × 1″ long (see page 91)
- Prepared 7″ × 9″ shield-shaped plaque (see page 90)

CROCHETING THE EARS

(make 2)

Cut two 14"-long pieces of the tan yarn and set them aside for later.

Setup: Using the tan yarn, ch 2, 6 sc in 2nd chain from hook. (Place a split-ring stitch marker to mark beginning of each round in the pattern, and move this marker up as you work each round.)

Rnd 1: 2 sc in each st around. Pull tail tight to close hole. (12 sc)

Rnd 2: *Sc in next st, 2 sc in next st; repeat from * around. (18 sc)

Rnd 3: *Sc in next 2 sts, 2 sc in next st; repeat from * around. (24 sc)

Rnd 4: *Sc in next 3 sts, 2 sc in next st; repeat from * around. (30 sc)

Rnd 5: *Sc in next 4 sts, 2 sc in next st; repeat from * around. (36 sc)

Rnd 6: *Sc in next 5 sts, 2 sc in next st; repeat from * around. (42 sc)

Rnd 7: *Sc in next 6 sts, 2 sc in next st; repeat from * around. (48 sc)

Closing the Ear

Slipstitch in first stitch of round, cut yarn, leaving a 12"-long tail for later use, and draw the tail through the loop on the hook to fasten off. Follow the instructions for the folded disk ear in A Variety of Ears on page 86 to prepare the ear for attachment later.

CROCHETING THE ANTLERS

The antlers are formed with multiple "points" that are whipstitched together when complete to make an impressive rack. Use the light gray yarn for all of the points.

Making the Short Points *(make 2)*

Setup: Using the light gray yarn, ch 2, 6 sc in 2nd chain from hook.

Rnd 1: 2 sc in each st around. Pull tail tight to close hole. (12 sc)

Rnds 2–10: Sc in each st around. (12 sc)

Slipstitch in first stitch of round, cut yarn, leaving a 12"-long tail for later use, and draw the tail through the loop on the hook to fasten off. Stuff firmly to the top with fiberfill.

Making the Long Points *(make 2)*

Setup: Using the light gray yarn, ch 2, 6 sc in 2nd chain from hook.

Rnd 1: 2 sc in each st around. Pull tail tight to close hole. (12 sc)

Rnds 2–15: Sc in each st around. (12 sc)

Stuff firmly to the top with fiberfill.

COMPLETING THE ANTLERS

Position one of the short points alongside one of the long points. (For a detail of what this should look like, see the Monumental Moose instructions, page 108.) Using a length of light gray yarn, whipstitch the two pieces together, connecting 2 stitches from each point. Draw the yarn through the last stitch to fasten off, weave in the tail, and trim off any extra yarn. Repeat with the other pair of points.

Rnd 1: Rejoin the light gray yarn and sc in each st around the edge, decreasing 1 st at the joints where the two points meet on each side by sc2tog at the joint (1 stitch from the first point and 1 stitch from its partner). (18 sc)

Rnds 2–25: Strap in — this will be a long journey. Sc in each st around. Stuff the antler as you go. (18 sc; when complete, the antler

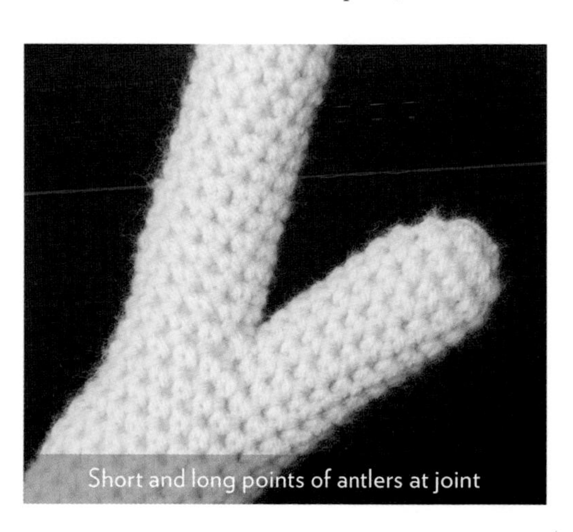
Short and long points of antlers at joint

will be about 10" long from top to bottom)

Complete stuffing the antlers all the way to the opening.

Rnd 26: Following the instructions for Changing the Yarn Color on page 82, switch to the tan yarn, and sc in each st around. (18 sc)

Slipstitch in first stitch of round, cut yarn, leaving a 12"-long tail for later use, and draw the tail through the loop on the hook to fasten off.

CROCHETING THE HEAD

Setup: Using the tan yarn, ch 2, 6 sc in 2nd chain from hook. Don't pull tail tight; leave a small hole where you can later insert the nose.

Rnd 1: 2 sc in each ch around. (12 sc)

Rnd 2: *Sc in next st, 2 sc in next st; repeat from * around. (18 sc)

Rnd 3: *Sc in next 2 sts, 2 sc in next st; repeat from * around. (24 sc)

Attaching the Nose

Position the nose as shown on the facing page and follow the instructions under Creating Faces, pages 84–85, to attach it securely.

Rnds 4–10: Sc in each st around, stuffing with fiberfill as you go. (24 sc)

Rnd 11: *Sc in next 10 sts, sc2tog; repeat from * around. (22 sc)

Rnd12: Sc in each st around. (22 sc)

Rnd 13: *Sc in next st, 2 sc in next st; repeat from * around. (33 sc)

Rnd 14: Sc in each st around. (33 sc)

Rnd 15: *Sc in next 2 sts, 2 sc in next st; repeat from * around. (44 sc)

Rnd 16: Sc in each st around. (44 sc)

Rnd 17: *Sc in next 3 sts, 2 sc in next st; repeat from * around. (55 sc)

Rnd 18: Sc in each st around. (55 sc)

Rnd 19: *Sc in next 4 sts, 2 sc in next st; repeat from * around. (66 sc)

Rnd 20: Sc in each st around. (66 sc)

Attaching the Eyes and Creating Sleepy Eyelids

Position the eyes as shown, and follow the directions for Creating Faces on pages 84–85 to attach them securely. To create the eyelids, thread a 14" length of the tan yarn into a yarn needle, and follow the directions for Sleepy-Eye Technique on page 87.

Rnd 21: *Sc in next 4 sts, sc2tog; repeat from * around. (55 sc)

Rnds 22 and 23: Sc in each st around. (55 sc)

Rnd 24: *Sc in next 3 sts, sc2tog; repeat from * around. (44 sc)

Stuff with fiberfill about halfway to the top.

Rnd 25: *Sc in next 2 sts, sc2tog; repeat from * around. (33 sc)

Rnd 26: *Sc in next st, sc2tog; repeat from * around. (22 sc)

Stuff all the way to the top, and insert the precut, predrilled dowel rod with the screw hole facing out (see pages 88–89). Add more stuffing around the dowel, if necessary to hold it firmly in place.

Rnd 27: *Sc, skip the next st, sc in the next st; repeat from * around, sc in last st. (15 sc)

Rnd 28: *Sc, skip the next st; repeat from * around. (8 sc)

Slipstitch in first stitch of round, cut yarn, leaving a 6"-long tail, draw the tail through the loop on the hook to fasten off, and weave it in on the wrong side.

Attaching the Antlers and Ears

Position the antlers on top of the head just above the eyes, with the longer points facing in toward each other as shown on page 96. Use the long tail of yarn to whipstitch the first antler securely to the head. Repeat with the second antler, adding extra stuffing if needed. Whipstitch the ears in place directly in front of the antlers. Fasten off yarn and weave in any loose ends.

MOUNTING

See Mounting Your Critter's Head, beginning on page 89, for instructions on how to complete your taxidermy head.

Sly Fox

Finished Measurements

- 5″ wide × 5″ long × 4″ deep

Hook

- US F/5 (3.75 mm) crochet hook

Yarn

- Worsted weight; 1 skein each of white and burnt orange (4)

Other Supplies

- One 20 mm smooth black plastic animal safety nose
- Two 12 mm brown plastic animal safety eyes
- Split-ring stitch marker
- Yarn needle
- Fiberfill
- Precut, predrilled dowel: 2″ diameter × 1″ long (see page 91)
- Prepared 5″ × 7″ shield-shaped plaque (see page 90)

CROCHETING THE EARS

(make 2)

Setup: Using the white yarn, ch 2, 6 sc in 2nd chain from hook. (Place a split-ring stitch marker to mark beginning of each round in the pattern, and move this marker up as you work each round.)

Rnd 1: 2 sc in each ch around. Pull tail tight to close hole. (12 sc)

Rnds 2 and 3: Sc in each st around. (12 sc)

Following the instructions for Changing the Yarn Color on page 82, switch to the burnt-orange yarn.

Rnd 4: Sc in each st around. (12 sc)

Rnd 5: *Sc in next st, 2 sc in next st; repeat from * around. (18 sc)

Rnds 6–9: Sc in each st around. (18 sc)

Rnd 10: *Sc in next st, sc2tog; repeat from * around. (12 sc)

Slipstitch in first stitch of round, cut yarn, leaving a 12"-long tail for later use, and draw the tail through the loop on the hook to fasten off. Flatten the tube and use the long tail to sew the opening closed. (See tube ear in A Variety of Ears, page 86, for an illustration of how to do this.)

CROCHETING THE NOSE AND HEAD

Setup: Using the white yarn, ch 2, 6 sc in 2nd chain from hook. Do not pull the tail tight; leave a small hole where you can later insert the nose.

Rnd 1: 2 sc in each st around. (12 sts)

Rnd 2: *Sc in next st, 2 sc in next st; repeat from * around. (18 sts)

Rnds 3 and 4: Sc 1 in each sc around. (18 sts)

Rnd 5: *Sc in next 7 sts, sc2tog; repeat from * around. (16 sc)

Rnds 6 and 7: Sc in each st around. (16 sc)

Attaching the Nose

Position the nose as shown below, and follow the instructions under Creating Faces on pages 84–85 to attach securely. Stuff firmly to the top with fiberfill.

Switch to the burnt-orange yarn and pull a loop through the back to the front and ch 2. (This counts as your first sc. After several rounds, securely weave in the beginning tail of the burnt-orange yarn.)

Rnd 1: *Sc in next st, 2 sc in next st; repeat from * around. (24 sc)

Rnd 2: *Sc in next 2 sts, 2 sc in next st; repeat from * around. (32 sc)

Rnd 3: *Sc in next 3 sts, 2 sc in next st; repeat from * around. (40 sc)

Rnd 4: *Sc in next 4 sts, 2 sc in next st; repeat from * around. (48 sc)

Rnd 5: *Sc in next 5 sts, 2 sc in next sc; repeat from * around. (56 sc)

Attaching the Eyes

Position the eyes right above the base of the nose/snout as shown on page 101, and follow the directions under Creating Faces on pages 84–85 to attach them securely.

Rnd 6: Sc in each st around. (56 sc)

Rnd 7: *Sc in next 6 sts, sc2tog; repeat from * around. (49 sc)

Rnd 8: *Sc in next 5 sts, sc2tog; repeat from * around. (42 sc)

Rnds 9 and 10: Sc in each st around. (42 sc)

Rnd 11: *Sc in next 4 sts, sc2tog; repeat from * around. (35 sc)

Rnd 12: *Sc in next 3 sts, sc2tog; repeat from * around. (28 sc)

Stuff with fiberfill about halfway to the top.

Rnd 13: *Sc in next 2 sts, sc2tog. (21 sc)

Stuff firmly to the top with fiberfill. Pop in the precut, predrilled dowel with the screw hole facing out (see pages 88–89). Add more stuffing around the dowel, if necessary, to hold it firmly in place. Now let's close up this fox!

Rnd 14: *Sc in next st, sc2tog; repeat from * around. (14 sc)

Rnd 15: *Sc in next st, skip next st; repeat from * around. (7 sc)

Slipstitch in first stitch of round, cut yarn, leaving a 6"-long tail, draw the tail through the loop on the hook to fasten off, and weave it in on the wrong side.

Attaching the Ears

For a perky look, position the ears about 7 rounds back from the base of the nose as shown on page 101. Use matching yarn to whipstitch the ears securely to the head, draw yarn through last stitch to fasten off. Weave in any loose tails on the wrong side.

MOUNTING

See Mounting Your Critter's Head, beginning on page 89, for instructions on how to complete your taxidermy head.

Rowdy Raccoon

Finished Measurements
- 6½″ wide × 5″ long × 4″ deep

Hook
- US F/5 (3.75 mm) crochet hook

Yarn
- Worsted weight; 1 skein each of black and medium gray

Other Supplies
- One 20 mm smooth black plastic animal safety nose
- Two 12 mm clear plastic animal safety eyes
- Split-ring stitch marker
- Yarn needle
- Fiberfill
- Precut, predrilled dowel: 2″ diameter × 1″ long (see page 91)
- Prepared 5″ × 7″ shield-shaped plaque (see page 90)

CROCHETING THE EARS
(make 2)

Setup: Using the black yarn, ch 2, 6 sc in 2nd chain from hook. (Place a split-ring stitch marker to mark beginning of each round in the pattern, and move this marker up as you work each round.)

Rnd 1: 2 sc in each st around. Pull tail tight to close hole. (12 sc)

Rnds 2 and 3: Sc in each st around. (12 sc)

Following the instructions for Changing the Yarn Color on page 82, switch to the medium gray yarn.

Rnd 4: Pull a loop through the inside of the ear to the front. Sc in each st around. (12 sc)

Rnd 5: *Sc in next st, 2 sc in next st; repeat from * around. (18 sc)

Rnds 6–9: Sc in each st around. (18 sc)

Rnd 10: *Sc in next st, sc2tog; repeat from * around. (12 sc)

Slipstitch in first stitch of round, cut yarn, leaving a 12"-long tail for later use, and draw the tail through the loop on the hook to fasten off. Flatten the tube and use the long tail to sew the opening closed. (See tube ear in A Variety of Ears, page 86, for an illustration of how to do this.)

CROCHETING THE NOSE AND HEAD

Setup: Using the medium gray yarn, ch 2, 6 sc in 2nd chain from hook. Don't pull tail tight; leave a small hole where you can later insert the nose.

Rnd 1: 2 sc in each st around. (12 sts)

Rnd 2: *Sc in next st, 2 sc in next st; repeat from * around. (18 sts)

Rnds 3 and 4: Sc in each st around. (18 sts)

Rnd 5: *Sc in next 7 sts, sc2tog; repeat from * around. (16 sc)

Rnds 6 and 7: Sc in each st around. (16 sc)

Attaching the Nose

Position the nose as shown on the facing page and follow the instructions under Creating Faces on pages 84–85 to attach it securely. Stuff firmly to the top with fiberfill.

Switch to the black yarn and pull a loop through from the back of the nose to the front and ch 2 (this counts as your first sc).

Rnd 8: *Sc in next st, 2 sc in next st; repeat from * around. (24 sc)

Rnd 9: *Sc in next 2 sts, 2 sc in next sc; repeat from * around. (32 sc)

Rnd 10: *Sc in next 3 sts, 2 sc in next st; repeat from * around. (40 sc)

Rnd 11: *Sc in next 4 sts, 2 sc in next st; repeat from * around. (48 sc)

Switch to the medium gray yarn.

Rnd 12: *Sc in next 5 sts, 2 sc in next st; repeat from * around. (56 sc)

Attaching the Eyes

Position the eyes above the base of the nose as shown, and follow the instructions under Creating Faces, pages 84–85, to attach them securely.

Switch to the medium gray yarn.

Rnd 13: Sc in each st around. (56 sc)

Rnds 14 and 15: *Sc in next 6 sts, sc2tog; repeat from * around. (42 sc after rnd 15)

Rnds 16 and 17: Sc in each st around. (42 sc)

Rnd 18: *Sc in next 4 sts, sc2tog; repeat from * around. (35 sc)

Rnd 19: *Sc in next 3 sts, sc2tog; repeat from * around. (28 sc)

Stuff with fiberfill about halfway to the top.

Rnd 20: *Sc in next 2 sts, sc2tog; repeat from * around. (21 sc)

Stuff firmly to the top with fiberfill. Pop in the precut, predrilled dowel with the screw hole facing out (see pages 88–89). Add more stuffing around the dowel, if necessary, to hold it firmly in place.

Rnd 21: *Sc in next st, sc2tog; repeat from * around. (14 sc)

Rnd 22: *Sc in next st, skip next st; repeat from * around. (7 sc)

Slipstitch in first stitch of round, cut yarn, leaving a 6"-long tail, draw the tail through the loop on the hook to fasten off, and weave it in on the wrong side.

Attaching the Ears

I usually position the ears about 7 rounds back from the base of the nose. Use whipstitches to attach them securely, and draw yarn through last stitch to fasten off. Weave in any loose ends.

MOUNTING

See Mounting Your Critter's Head, beginning on page 89, for instructions on how to complete your taxidermy head.

Monumental Moose

Finished Measurements

- 18½" wide × 12" long × 11" deep

Hook

- US F/5 (3.75 mm) crochet hook

Yarn

- Worsted weight; 1 skein each of brown and tan

Other Supplies

- Two 18 mm clear plastic animal safety eyes
- Split-ring stitch marker
- Yarn needle
- Fiberfill
- Precut, predrilled dowel: 4"-diameter circle cut from a 1 × 6 pine board (see A Large Exception, page 91)
- Prepared 11½" × 8½" scalloped plaque (see page 90)

CROCHETING THE EYE ROUNDIES

(make 2)

Setup: Using the brown yarn, ch 2, 6 sc into the 2nd ch from hook. Don't pull tail tight; leave a small hole where you can later insert the eye. (Place a split-ring stitch marker to mark beginning of each round in the pattern, and move this marker up as you work each round.)

Rnd 1: *2 sc in each st around.* (12 sc)

Slipstitch in first stitch of round, cut yarn, leaving a 12"-long tail for later use, and draw the tail through the loop on the hook to fasten off.

CROCHETING THE NOSE ROUNDIES

(make 2)

Setup: Using the brown yarn, ch 2, 6 sc in 2nd chain from the hook.

Rnd 1: 2 sc in each st around. Pull tail tight to close hole. (12 sc)

Slipstitch in first stitch of round, cut yarn, leaving a 12"-long tail for later use, and draw the tail through the loop on the hook to fasten off.

CROCHETING THE EARS

(make 2)

Setup: Using the brown yarn, ch 2, 6 sc in 2nd chain from the hook.

Rnd 1: *2 sc in each st around. Pull tail tight to close hole. (12 sc)

Rnd 2: *Sc in next st, 2 sc in next st; repeat from * around. (18 sc)

Rnd 3: *Sc in next 2 sts, 2 sc in next st; repeat from * around. (24 sc)

Rnd 4: *Sc in next 3 sts, 2 sc in next st; repeat from * around. (30 sc)

Rnd 5: *Sc in next 4 sts, 2 sc in next st; repeat from * around. (36 sc)

Rnd 6: *Sc in next 5 sts, 2 sc next st; repeat from * around. (42 sc)

Rnd 7: *Sc in next 6 sts, 2 sc next st; repeat from * around. (48 sc)

Rnd 8: *Sc in next 7 sts, 2 sc next st; repeat from * around. (54 sc)

Rnd 9: *Sc in next 8 sts, 2 sc in next st; repeat from * around. (60 sc)

Closing the Ear

Slipstitch in first stitch of round, cut yarn, leaving a 12"-long tail for later use, and draw the tail through the loop on the hook to fasten off. Follow the instructions for the folded disk ear in A Variety of Ears on page 86 to prepare the ear for attachment later. *Note:* Because of the way you increased, the disk is hexagonal. Fold the ear so that the points align. When you sew the ear partially closed, begin at the fold and stitch across half of one of the six sides and then across the next whole side, leaving one and one-half sides open (see photo).

CROCHETING THE RACK

(make 2)

The moose's rack is made up of six nubs, four of which are sewn together in pairs and two are left single. Each of the singles is sewn to a paired nub after they are stuffed.

Setup: Using the tan yarn, ch 2, 6 sc in 2nd chain from hook.

Rnd 1: 2 sc in each st around. Pull tail tight to close hole. (12 sc)

Rnd 2: *Sc in next st, 2 sc in next st; repeat from * around. (18 sc)

Rnds 3–7: Sc in each st around. (18 sc)

Stuff with fiberfill about halfway to the top.

Rnd 8: *Sc in next st, sc2tog; repeat from * around. (12 sc)

Rnd 9: Sc in each st around. (12 sc)

Slipstitch in first stitch of round, cut yarn, leaving a 12"-long tail for later use, and draw the tail through the loop on the hook to fasten off. Stuff all the way to the top.

Joining the Nubs

Position two of the completed nubs side by side as shown on the next page. Whipstitch the two pieces together, joining 2 stitches from each nub. Draw your yarn through the last stitch to fasten off and weave in loose end. (20 sc remain open, 10 sc from each small nub) Repeat with two other nubs. You now

Two nubs whipstitched together to begin crocheting the new opening (A)

Crocheting around two joined nubs (B)

Whipstitching third nub onto rack (C)

have two pairs of nubs that have been sewn together and two single, unattached nubs (four pieces in all).

Now we are going to join the whole moose rack, and this is where things get kind of tricky. Join a new length of the tan yarn to one of the joined nubs at the joint, just after your last whipstitch (A).

Rnd 10: *Sc in 9 sts around one of the nubs until you get to the joint, sc2tog at the joint (one stitch from the first nub and one stitch from its partner), sc in the next sts around the second nub, sc2tog at the joint (B), joining the last and first stitches of the round. (18 sc)

Rnds 11–14: Sc in each st around. (18 sc)

Stuff firmly to the top with fiberfill.

Position one of the single (unjoined) nubs as shown at left, and whipstitch about 1" along the edges to join the single nub to the larger piece, using 3 whipstitches (C). Draw the yarn through the last stitch and weave in the loose end.

Rnd 15: Beginning at the end of the whipstitching, sc in next 15 sts, sc2tog (at the joint), sc in the next 9 sts, sc2tog (at the joint). (26 sc)

Rnds 16–18: Sc in each st around, stuffing firmly with fiberfill as you work. (26 sc)

Rnd 19: *Sc in next 11 sts, sc2tog; repeat from * around (D). (24 sc)

Rnds 20–34: Sc in each st around. (24 sc)

Stuff firmly with fiberfill as you work.

Following the instructions under Changing the Yarn Color on page 82, switch to the brown yarn.

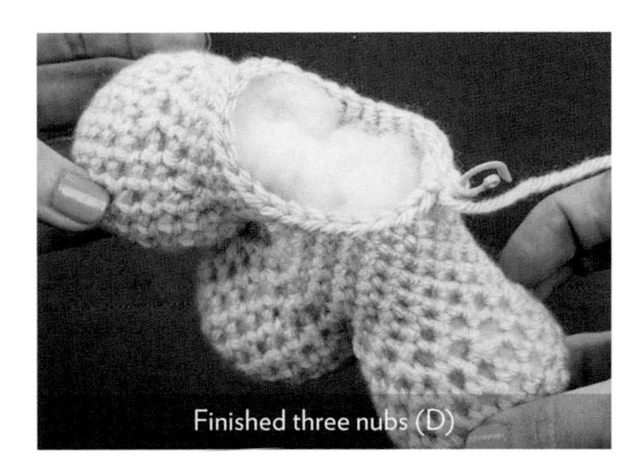
Finished three nubs (D)

Rnd 35: Sc in each st around, stuffing firmly with fiberfill as you work. (24 sc)

Slipstitch in first stitch of round, cut yarn, leaving a 12"-long tail for later use, and draw the tail through the loop on the hook to fasten off. Make sure this piece is stuffed all the way to the top.

Join the remaining single nub with the other joined pair as described above.

Crocheting the Head

Setup: Using the brown yarn, ch 2, 6 sc into 2nd chain from hook.

Rnd 1: *2 sc in each st around.* Pull tail tight to close hole. (12 sc)

Rnd 2: *Sc in next st, 2 sc into next st; repeat from * around. (18 sc)

Rnd 3: *Sc in next 2 sts, 2 sc in next st; repeat from * around. (24 sc)

Rnd 4: *Sc in next 3 sts, 2 sc in next st; repeat from * around. (30 sc)

Rnd 5: *Sc in next 4 sts, 2 in next st; repeat from * around. (36 sc)

Rnd 6: *Sc in next 5 sts, 2 sc in next st; repeat from * around. (42 sc)

Rnd 7: *Sc in next 6 sts, 2 sc next st; repeat from * around. (48 sc)

Attaching the Nose Roundies

Position the nose roundies equal widths apart in the middle of the moose's snout as shown on the next page, and whipstitch them securely in place.

Rnd 8: *Sc in the next 7 sts, 2 sc in the next st; repeat from * around. (54 sc)

Rnd 9: *Sc in the next 8 sts, 2 sc in the next st; repeat from * around. (60 sc)

Rnds 10–15: Sc in each st around. (60 sc)

Rnd 16: *Sc in next 8 sts, sc2tog; repeat from * around. (54 sc)

Rnd 17: *Sc in next 7 sts, sc2tog; repeat from * around. (48 sc)

Rnd 18: *Sc in next 6 sts, sc2tog; repeat from * around. (42 sc)

Rnd 19: *Sc in next 5 sts, sc2tog; repeat from * around. (36 sc)

Rnd 20: *Sc in next 4 sts, sc2tog; repeat from * around. (30 sc)

Rnds 21–35: Sc in each st around. (30 sc)

Rnd 36: *Sc in next 4 sts, 2 sc in next st; repeat from * around. (36 sc)

Rnd 37: *Sc in next 5 sts, 2 sc in next st; repeat from * around. (42 sc)

Rnd 38: *Sc in next 6 sts, 2 sc in next st; repeat from * around. (48 sc)

Rnd 39: *Sc in next 7 sts, 2 sc in next st; repeat from * around. (54 sc)

Rnd 40: *Sc in next 8 sts, 2 sc in next st; repeat from * around. (60 sc)

At this point you may be thinking, "What did I get myself into?" Take heart, because you're almost finished! This is the biggest and hardest pattern in the book, so if you can accomplish this, you can accomplish all the others.

Rnds 41–45: Sc in each st around. (60 sc)

Attaching the Eyes and Eye Roundies

Position the eyes and eye roundies an equal distance apart at the top of the head just above the base of the snout as shown, and follow the instructions under Creating Faces on pages 84–85, to attach them securely. Thread a yarn needle with matching yarn and whipstitch the eye roundies to the head, drawing the yarn through your last stitch to fasten off on the wrong side of the head. Weave in the tail.

Rnds 46–50: Sc in each st around. (60 sc)

Stuff firmly to the top with fiberfill.

Rnd 51: *Sc into next 8 sts, sc2tog; repeat from * around. (54 sc)

Rnd 52: *Sc in next 7 sts, sc2tog; repeat from * around. (48 sc)

Rnd 53: *Sc in next 6 sts, sc2tog; repeat from * around. (42 sc)

Stuff the head all the way to the top. Insert the precut, predrilled dowel into the head with the screw hole facing out (see pages 88–89). Add more stuffing around the dowel, if necessary, to hold it firmly in place. You're in the home stretch now — it's time to close up this moose!

Rnd 54: *Sc in next 5 sts, sc2tog; repeat from * around. (36 sc)

Rnd 55: *Sc in next 4 sts, sc2tog; repeat from * around. (30 sc)

Rnd 56: *Sc in next 3 sts, sc2tog; repeat from * around. (24 sc)

Rnd 57: *Sc in next 2 sts, sc2tog; repeat from * around. (18 sc)

Slipstitch in first stitch of round, cut yarn, leaving a 6"-long tail, draw the tail through the loop on the hook to fasten off, and weave it in on the wrong side.

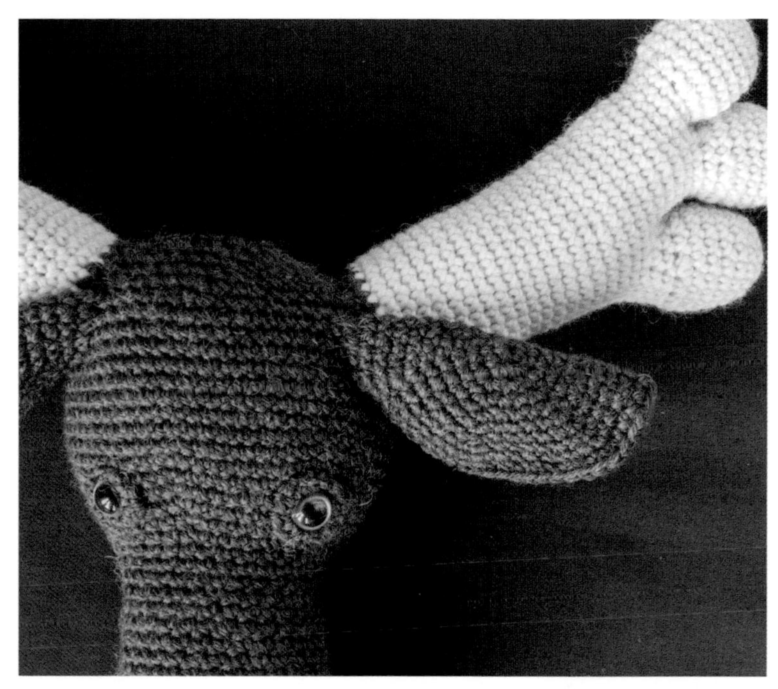

FINISHING TOUCHES

Attaching the Rack

Now it's that fun time when you attach the moose's rack to the head. You may want to stuff the rack pieces more thoroughly at this point. They should be firmly packed so that they are upright and not floppy.

Position one of the rack pieces at the top of the head just above one of the eyes. The third small nub should be on the outside of both racks (see photo). Use whipstitches to sew the rack in place, draw yarn through the last stitch at the back of the head to fasten off, and weave in the ends. Repeat with the second rack.

Note: Take extra care to position the two parts of the rack so that they are exact mirror images of one another. I've sewn on my rack only to find out later that I sewed them on incorrectly and then had to redo them, which is no fun!

Attaching the Ears

Position one ear right in front of each part of the rack, whipstitching them directly into the round in front of the rack. Draw your yarn through the last stitch to fasten off, trim yarn, and weave in the tail on the wrong side.

Creating the Chin Scruff

It's time to add the final touch to your moose — the chin scruff! Cut ten 12"-long pieces of the brown yarn. To create the scruff, fold each length of yarn in half and use a crochet hook to draw the folded end through the fabric at the chin, as shown below. When you have a little loop, draw the cut ends through the loop and pull tight, just like making fringe on a scarf. After you've attached as much yarn as you want for your scruff, you may want to give it a little trim (or you can leave it long, if you prefer). Take all the pieces of yarn in your hand, as though you were trimming someone's hair, and cut the scruff into a V shape.

MOUNTING

See Mounting Your Critter's Head, beginning on page 89, for instructions on how to complete your taxidermy head.

Now, give yourself a pat on the back, because you have just completed the most involved pattern in the book!

Creating the chin scruff

Brown Bear

Finished Measurements

- 6½″ wide × 6″ long × 4½″ deep

Hook

- US F/5 (3.75 mm) crochet hook

Yarn

- Worsted weight; 1 skein of brown

Other Supplies

- One 20 mm textured black plastic animal safety nose
- Two 15 mm yellow plastic animal safety eyes (you may use brown, if you prefer)
- Split-ring stitch marker
- Yarn needle
- Fiberfill
- Precut, predrilled dowel: 2″ diameter × 1″ long (see page 91)
- Prepared 7″ square plaque (see page 90)

CROCHETING THE EYE ROUNDIES

(make 2)

Setup: Ch 2, 6 sc into 2nd chain from the hook. Don't pull tail tight; leave a small hole where you can later insert the eye. (Place a split-ring stitch marker to mark beginning of each round in the pattern, and move this marker up as you work each round.)

Rnd 1: 2 sc in each st around. (12 sc)

Cut yarn, leaving a 12"-long tail, and draw the tail through the last stitch to fasten off. You will use the tail later to sew the eye roundies onto the head.

CROCHETING THE EARS

(make 2)

Setup: Ch 2, 6 sc into 2nd chain from hook.

Rnd 1: 2 sc in each st around. Pull tail tight to close hole. (12 sc)

Rnd 2: *Sc into next st, 2 sc in next st; repeat from * around. (18 sc)

Rnds 3–5: Sc in each st around. (18 sc)

Rnd 6: *Sc in next 7 sts, sc2tog; repeat from * around. (16 sc)

Rnd 7: Sc in each st around. (16 sc)

Closing the Ear

Slipstitch in first stitch of round, cut yarn, leaving a 12"-long tail for later use, and draw the tail through the loop on the hook to fasten off. Flatten the tube and use the long tail to sew the opening closed. (See the tube ear in A Variety of Ears on page 86 for an illustration of how to do this.)

CROCHETING THE FACE

Setup: Ch 2, 6 sc into 2nd chain from hook. Don't pull the tail tight; leave a small hole where you can later insert the nose.

Rnd 1: 2 sc in each st around. (12 sc)

Rnd 2: *Sc in next st, 2 sc in next st; repeat from * around. (18 sc)

Rnds 3–8: Sc in each st around. (18 sc)

Attaching the Nose

Position the nose as shown on the facing page, and follow the instructions under Creating Faces on pages 84–85 to attach it securely. Stuff nose all the way to the top.

Rnd 9: *Sc in next st, 2 sc next st; repeat from * around. (27 sc)

Rnd 10: *Sc in next 2 sts, 2 sc in next st; repeat from * around. (36 sc)

Rnd 11: *Sc in next 3 sts, 2 sc next st; repeat from * around. (45 sc)

Rnd 12: *Sc in next 4 sts, 2 sc in next st; repeat from * around. (54 sc)

Rnd 13: *Sc in next 5 sts, 2 sc in next st; repeat from * around. (63 sc)

Rnd 14: *Sc in next 6 sts, 2 sc in next st; repeat from * around. (72 sc)

Attaching the Eyes and Eye Roundies

Position the eyes and eye roundies just above the base of the nose as shown, and follow the instructions under Creating Faces to attach them securely.

CROCHETING THE HEAD

Rnd 15: *Sc in next 6 sts, sc2tog; repeat from * around. (63 sc)

Rnd 16: *Sc in next 5 sts, sc2tog; repeat from * around. (54 sc)

Rnds 17 and 18: Sc in each st around. (54 sc)

Rnd 19: *Sc in next 4 sts, sc2tog; repeat from * around. (45 sc)

Rnd 20: *Sc in next 3 sts, sc2tog; repeat from * around. (36 sc)

Stuff with fiberfill about halfway to the top.

Rnd 21: *Sc in next 2 sts, sc2tog*; repeat from * around. (27 sc)

Rnd 22: *Sc in next st, sc2tog; repeat from * around. (18 sc)

Stuff firmly to the top with fiberfill. Pop in the precut, predrilled dowel with the screw hole facing out (see pages 88–89). Add more stuffing around the dowel, if necessary to hold it firmly in place.

Rnd 23: *Sc in next st, skip the next st; repeat from * around. (9 sc)

Slipstitch in first stitch of round, cut

yarn, leaving a 6"-long tail, draw the tail through the loop on the hook to fasten off, and weave it in on the wrong side.

Attaching the Ears

For a perky, alert expression on your bear's face, position the ears about 3 rounds back and just above the eye roundies, and use matching yarn to whip-stitch the bottom edge securely to the head.

MOUNTING

See Mounting Your Critter's Head, beginning on page 89, for instructions on how to complete your taxidermy head.

Little Stinker

Finished Measurements
- 3½″ wide × 3″ long × 2¾″ deep

Hooks
- US F/5 (3.75 mm) crochet hook (for body)
- US D/3 (3.25 mm) crochet hook (for stripe)

Yarn
- Worsted weight; 1 skein of black (for body) 4
- Super-bulky faux fur or eyelash yarn; 1 skein of white (for stripe) 6

Other Supplies
- One 15 mm smooth black plastic animal safety nose
- Two 9 mm solid black plastic animal safety eyes
- Split-ring stitch marker
- Yarn needle
- Fiberfill
- Precut, predrilled dowel: 1¼″ diameter × 1″ long (see page 91)
- Prepared 4″ square plaque (see page 90)

CROCHETING THE EARS

(make 2)

Setup: Using the US F/5 (3.75 mm) hook and black yarn, ch 2, 6 sc into 2nd chain from hook. (Place a split-ring marker to mark the beginning of each round in the pattern, and move this marker up as you work each round.)

Rnd 1: 2 sc in each st around. Pull tail tight to close hole. (12 sc)

Slipstitch in first stitch of round, cut yarn, leaving a 12"-long tail for later use, and draw the tail through the loop on the hook to fasten off. Weave in the beginning tail. (Do not fold ear.)

CROCHETING THE HEAD

Setup: Using the US F/5 (3.75 mm) hook and black yarn, ch 2, 6 sc into 2nd chain from hook. Don't pull tail tight; leave a small hole where you can later insert the nose.

Rnd 1: 2 sc in each st around. (12 sc)

Rnds 2–3: Sc in each st around. (12 sc)

Rnd 4: 2 sc in each st around. (24 sc)

Rnds 5–10: Sc in each st around. (24 sc)

Attaching the Nose and Eyes

Position the nose as shown on the facing page, and attach it securely, following instructions under Creating Faces on pages 84–85. Position the eyes a few rounds back from the nose where the head starts to develop as shown, and attach them securely.

FINISHING TOUCHES

Crocheting the Stripe

Get out that fluffy, white faux fur yarn and your US D/3 (3.25 mm) hook. Fold the head in half as shown below. Starting just above or even between the eyes, pull a loop of the white yarn through an open stitch. Working from front to back, 8 sc in each open stitch. (For advice about working with the faux fur yarn, see Here Comes the Fuzz, page 88.)

Slipstitch in the last stitch, cut yarn, leaving a short tail, and pull the tail through to fasten off. Weave in both tails and trim off excess yarn. Fluff the white yarn with your fingers to comb out the stripe. Now I'll bet your little skunk is looking really skunky! Stuff the head almost all the way to the top.

Rnd 11: Again using the US F/5 (3.75 mm) hook and the black yarn, go back to where

Crocheting faux fur into folded head

you left off crocheting the body, and *sc in next st, sc2tog; repeat from * around. (16 sc)

Stuff the skunk head the rest of the way, and insert your precut, pre-drilled dowel with the screw hole facing out (see pages 88–89). Add more stuffing around the dowel, if necessary, to hold it firmly in place.

Rnd 12: *Sc in next st, skip next st; repeat from * around. (8 sc)

Slipstitch in first stitch of round, cut yarn, leaving a 6"-long tail, draw the tail through the loop on the hook to fasten off, and weave it in on the wrong side.

Attaching the Ears

Last but not least, position the ears about 7 rounds back from the nose and 2 rounds behind the eyes, as shown below and use whipstitches to sew them to the head. Draw the yarn through the last stitch to fasten off, and weave in any excess yarn on the wrong side.

MOUNTING

See Mounting Your Critter's Head, beginning on page 89, for instructions on how to complete your taxidermy head.

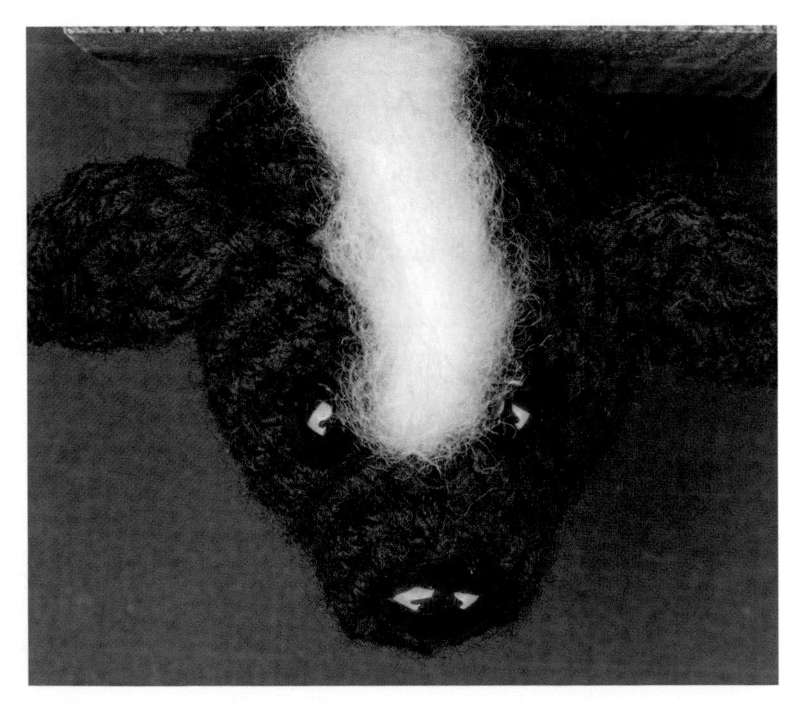

Meek Mouse

Finished Measurements

- 3″ wide × 3″ long × 2¾″ deep

Hook

- US F/5 (3.75 mm) crochet hook

Yarn

- Worsted weight; 1 skein each of light pink and silver gray

Other Supplies

- One 15 mm smooth black plastic animal nose
- Two 9 mm solid black plastic animal safety eyes
- Split-ring stitch marker
- Yarn needle
- Fiberfill
- Precut, predrilled dowel: 1¼″ diameter × 1″ long (see page 91)
- Prepared 4″ round plaque (see page 90)

CROCHETING THE EARS

(make 2)

Setup: Using the light pink yarn, ch 2, 6 sc into 2nd chain from hook. (Place a split-ring stitch marker to mark beginning of each round in the pattern, and move this marker up as you work each round.)

Rnd 1: 2 sc in each st around. Pull tail tight to close hole. (12 sc)

Slipstitch in first stitch of round, cut yarn, leaving a 12"-long tail for later use, and draw the tail through the loop on the hook to fasten off. Weave in the beginning tail and cut off the excess. (Do not fold ear.)

CROCHETING THE HEAD

Setup: Using the yarn you've chosen for the body, ch 2, 6 sc into 2nd chain from hook. Don't pull tail tight; leave a small hole where you can later insert the nose.

Rnd 1: 2 sc in each st around. (12 sc)

Rnds 2 and 3: Sc in each st around. (12 sc)

Rnd 4: 2 sc in each st around. (24 sc)

Rnds 5–11: Sc in each st around. (24 sc)

Attaching the Nose and Eyes

Position the nose and eyes as shown at right, and attach them to the head following the instructions under Creating Faces on pages 84–85. Stuff the head halfway to the top.

Rnd 12: *Sc in next st, sc2tog; repeat from * around. (18 sc)

Stuff the head the rest of the way, and insert your precut, predrilled dowel with the screw hole facing out (see pages 88–89). Add more stuffing around the dowel, if necessary, to hold it firmly in place.

Rnd 13: *Sc in next st, skip the next st; repeat from * around. (12 sc)

Slipstitch in first stitch of round, cut yarn, leaving a 6"-long tail, draw the tail through the loop on the hook to fasten off, and weave it in on the wrong side.

Attaching the Ears

Last but not least, attach the ears to the head. Position them about 7 rounds back from the nose and 2 rounds behind the eyes, and whipstitch them in place. Draw the yarn through the last stitch to fasten off, weave in yarn tails, and trim excess.

MOUNTING

See Mounting Your Critter's Head, beginning on page 89, for instructions on how to complete your taxidermy head.

Mallard Duck

Finished Measurements
- 3″ wide × 3″ long × 7″ deep

Hook
- US F/5 (3.75 mm) crochet hook

Yarn
- Worsted weight; 1 skein each of gold, dark olive green, white, and brown

Other Supplies
- Two 12 mm yellow plastic animal safety eyes
- Split-ring stitch marker
- Yarn needle
- Fiberfill
- Precut, predrilled dowel: 1¼″ diameter × 2″ long (see page 91)
- Prepared 4″ round plaque (see page 90)

CROCHETING THE BILL AND HEAD

Setup: Using the gold yarn, ch 2, 6 sc into 2nd chain from the hook. (Place a split-ring stitch marker to mark beginning of each round in the pattern, and move this marker up as you work each round.)

Rnd 1: 2 sc in each st around. Pull tail tight to close hole. (12 sc)

Rnds 2–12: Sc in each st around. (12 sc) Stuff firmly with fiberfill as you work.

Following the instructions for Changing the Yarn Color on page 82, switch to the dark olive-green yarn.

Rnd 13: 2 sc in each st around. (24 sc)

Rnds 14–21: Sc in each st around. (24 sc)

Attaching the Eyes

Position the eyes as shown below, and

attach them securely to the head following the instructions under Creating Faces on pages 84–85.

Rnd 22: *Sc in next 4 sts, sc2tog; repeat from * around. (20 sc)

Rnd 23: *Sc in next 2 sts, sc2tog; repeat from * around. (15 sc)

Rnd 24: Sc in each st around. (15 sc)

Switch to the white yarn.

Rnds 25 and 26: Sc in each st around, stuffing firmly with fiberfill as you work. (15 sc)

Switch to the brown yarn. Leave a long tail of the white yarn and pull it through to the front for later use. Weave in the brown tail on the wrong side.

Rnds 27–31: Sc in each st around. (15 sc)

Insert the precut, predrilled dowel into the duck's neck with the screw hole facing out (see pages 88–89). Add more stuffing around the dowel, if necessary, to hold it firmly in place.

Rnd 32: *Sc in next st, skip 1 st; repeat from * around. (8 sc)

Slipstitch in first stitch of round, cut yarn, leaving a 6"-long tail, draw the tail through the loop on the hook to fasten off, and weave it in on the wrong side.

MOUNTING

See Mounting Your Critter's Head, beginning on page 89, for instructions on how to complete your taxidermy head.

Little Hooter

Finished Measurements

- 4″ wide × 4″ long × 2½″ deep

Hook

- US F/5 (3.75 mm) crochet hook

Yarn

- *For white owl (photo on page 1):* worsted weight; 1 skein white and about 2 yards of gold (for beak)

- *For brown owl:* worsted weight; 1 skein each of brown and tan and about 2 yards of orange (for beak)

Other Supplies

- Two 16 mm clear plastic animal safety eyes
- Split-ring stitch marker
- Yarn needle
- Fiberfill
- Precut, predrilled dowel: 2″ diameter × 1″ long (see page 91)
- Prepared 5″ square or round plaque (see page 90)

Note: The directions that follow are for the brown owl; use all white yarn for the white owl (see page 1), with gold for its beak.

CROCHETING THE EYE ROUNDIES

(make 2)

Setup: Using the tan yarn, ch 2, 6 sc in 2nd chain from hook. Don't pull tail tight; leave a small hole where you can later insert the eyes. (Place a split-ring stitch marker to mark beginning of each round in the pattern, and move this marker up as you work each round.)

Rnd 1: 2 sc in each st around. (12 sc)

Slipstitch in first stitch of round, cut yarn, leaving a 12"-long tail for sewing on the eye roundies later.

CROCHETING THE HOOD

Setup: Using the brown yarn, ch 18. Turn.

Row 1: Sc into 2nd ch from hook, sc into next 16 ch. (17 sc) Ch 1 and turn.

Row 2: Skip first sc, sc in next 16 sts. (17 sc) Ch 1 and turn.

Continue to skip the first sc in each of the following rows through Row 16. *Note:* The turning chain counts as 1 sc.

Row 3: Sc in next 16 sts. (17 sc) Ch 1 and turn.

Row 4: Sc in next 15 sts. (16 sc) Ch 1 and turn.

Row 5: Sc in next 14 sts. (15 sc) Ch 1 and turn.

Row 6: Sc in next 13 sts. (14 sc) Ch 1 and turn.

Row 7: Sc in next 12 sts. (13 sc) Ch 1 and turn.

Row 8: Sc in next 11 sts. (12 sc) Ch 1 and turn.

Row 9: Sc in next 10 sts. (11 sc) Ch 1 and turn.

Row 10: Sc in next 9 sts. (10 sc) Ch 1 and turn.

Row 11: Sc in next 8 sts. (9 sc) Ch 1 and turn.

Row 12: Sc in next 7 sts. (8 sc) Ch 1 and turn.

Row 13: Sc in next 6 sts. (7 sc) Ch 1 and turn.

Row 14: Sc in next 5 sts. (6 sc) Ch 1 and turn.

Row 15: Sc in next 4 sts. (5 sc) Ch 1 and turn.

Row 16: Sc in next 3 sts. (4 sc) Chain 1.

Edging the hood: Sc in each available st all the way around the triangle. When you get to the corners, 2 sc in each corner st.

Slipstitch in first stitch of round, cut yarn, leaving a 12"-long tail for later use, and draw the tail through the loop on the hook to fasten off.

CROCHETING THE HEAD

Setup: Using the brown yarn, ch 2, 6 sc in 2nd chain from hook.

Rnd 1: 2 sc in each st around. Pull tail tight to close hole. (12 sc)

Rnd 2: *Sc in next st, 2 sc next st; repeat from * around. (18 sc)

Rnd 3: *Sc in next 2 sts, 2 sc in next st; repeat from * around. (24 sc)

Rnd 4: *Sc in next 3 sts, 2 sc in next st; repeat from * around. (30 sc)

Rnd 5: *Sc in next 4 sts, 2 sc in next st; repeat from * around. (36 sc)

Rnd 6: *Sc in next 5 sts, 2 sc in next st; repeat from * around. (42 sc)

Rnd 7: *Sc in next 6 sts, 2 sc in next st; repeat from * around. (48 sc)

Rnd 8: *Sc in next 6 sts, sc2tog; repeat from * around. (42 sc)

Attaching the Eyes and Eye Roundies

Position the eyes and eye roundies centered on the face, about 1" apart, and attach them, following the instructions under Creating Faces on pages 84–85.

Creating the Beak

Thread a 24" length of the orange yarn into a yarn needle. Insert the needle from the wrong side, and embroider a triangular-shaped beak, starting each stitch at the same point at the bottom of the beak and filling the entire area with vertical stitches of yarn (satin stitch) (A). Next, use horizontal stitches across the top of the beak, again placing the stitches close together so that you cover the entire area: about 5 stitches should do it (B). Vertically from top to bottom, the beak should measure about ¾" and, horizontally across the top, about 1". Draw yarn to the wrong side and fasten off. Weave in ends and trim any excess yarn.

Rnd 9: *Sc in the next 5 sts, sc2tog; repeat from * around. (36 sc)

Rnds 10 and 11: Sc in each st around. (36 sc)

Rnd 12: *Sc in next 4 sts, sc2tog; repeat from * around. (30 sc)

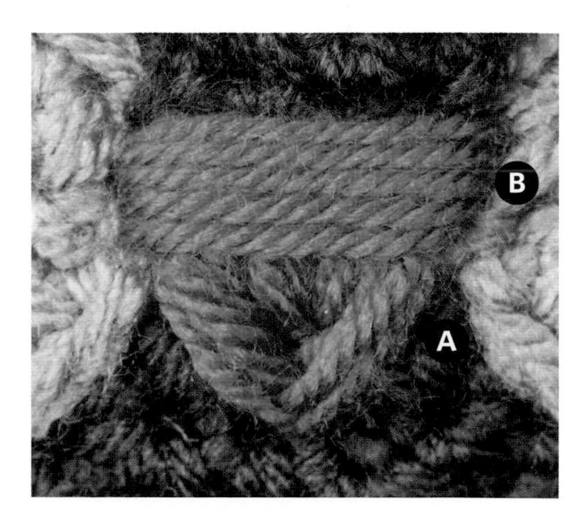

Stuff with fiberfill about halfway to the top.

Rnd 13: *Sc in the next 3 sts, sc2tog; repeat from * around. (24 sc)

Rnd 14: *Sc in the next 2 sts, sc2tog; repeat from * around. (18 sc) Push the precut, predrilled dowel into place with the screw hole facing out (see pages 88–89). Add more stuffing around the dowel, if necessary, to hold it firmly in place, and continue stuffing to the top.

Rnd 15: *Sc in next st, sc2tog; repeat from * around. (12 sc)

Slipstitch in first stitch of round, cut yarn, leaving a 6"-long tail, draw the tail through the loop on the hook to fasten off, and weave it in on the wrong side.

Attaching the Hood

Position the hood so that the short edge (the last row crocheted, which consists of 4 stitches) is flush with the top of the owl's beak; drape the rest of the hood over the back of the head. Thread a yarn needle with matching yarn and take small running stitches close to the edge of the hood to join it to the head all the way around. Try to make these stitches as invisible as possible. Cut the yarn, leaving a short tail. Draw the tail through the last stitch to fasten off and weave it in. Cut off excess yarn.

MOUNTING

See Mounting Your Critter's Head, beginning on page 89, for instructions on how to complete your taxidermy head.

You have just completed the cutest little hooter there ever was!

Pinky Pig

Finished Measurements

- 7″ wide × 5½″ long × 5½″ deep

Hook

- US F/5 (3.75 mm) crochet hook

Yarn

- Worsted weight; 1 skein of pale pink (4)

Other Supplies

- Two 12 mm clear plastic animal safety eyes
- Split-ring stitch marker
- Yarn needle
- Fiberfill
- Precut, predrilled dowel: 2″ diameter × 1″ long (see page 91)
- Prepared 7″ square plaque (see page 90)

Abbreviations

- **sc tbl** Single crochet through back loop only (see page 201)

CROCHETING THE EYE ROUNDIES

(make 2)

Setup: Ch 2, 6 sc into 2nd chain from hook. Don't pull tail tight; leave a small hole where you can later insert the eyes. (Place a split-ring stitch marker to mark beginning of each round in the pattern, and move this marker up as you work each round.)

Rnd 1: 2 sc in each st around. (12 sc)

Slipstitch in first stitch of round, cut yarn, leaving a 12"-long tail for later use, and draw the tail through the loop on the hook to fasten off.

CROCHETING THE NOSE ROUNDIES

(make 2)

Setup: Ch 2, 6 sc into 2nd chain from hook.

Rnd 1: 2 sc in each st around. Pull the tail

tight to close hole. (12 sc)

Slipstitch in first stitch of round, cut yarn, leaving a 12"-long tail for later use, and draw the tail through the loop on the hook to fasten off.

CROCHETING THE EARS

(make 2)

Setup: Ch 2, 6 sc into 2nd chain from the hook.

Rnd 1: 2 sc in each st around. Pull tail tight to close hole. (12 sc)

Rnd 2: *1 sc in next st, 2 sc in next st; repeat from * around. (18 sc)

Rnd 3: *Sc in next 2 sts, 2 sc in next st; repeat from * around. (24 sc)

Rnd 4: *Sc in next 3 sts, 2 sc in next st; repeat from * around. (30 sc)

Closing the Ear

Slipstitch in first stitch of round, cut yarn, leaving a 12"-long tail for later use, and draw the tail through the loop on the hook to fasten off. Follow the instructions for folded disk ears in A Variety of Ears on page 86 to prepare the ear for attachment later.

CROCHETING THE SNOUT

Setup: Ch 2, 6 sc into 2nd chain from the hook. (6 sc)

Rnd 1: 2 sc in each st around. Pull tail tight to close hole. (12 sc)

Rnd 2: *Sc in next st, 2 sc in next st; repeat from * around. (18 sc)

Rnd 3: *Sc in next 2 sts, 2 sc in next st; repeat from * around. (24 sc)

Rnd 4: *Sc in next 3 sts, 2 sc in next st; repeat from * around. (30 sc)

Rnd 5: *Sc in next 4 sts, 2 sc in next st; repeat from * around. (36 sc)

Rnd 6: Sc tbl in each st around. (36 sc)

Rnd 7: Sc in each st around. (36 sc)

Attaching the Nose Roundies

Position the nose roundies as shown on page 127, and whipstitch them securely in place.

Rnd 8: *Sc in next 4 sc, sc2tog; repeat from * around. (30 sc)

Rnd 9: Sc in each st around. (30 sc)

Rnd 10: *Sc in next 2 sts, sc2tog; repeat from * around. (24 sc)

Rnd 11: Sc in each st around. (24 sc)

Rnd 12: *Sc in next 2 sts, sc2tog; repeat from * around. (18 sc)

Rnds 13–15: Sc in each st around. (18 sc)

Stuff firmly to the top with fiberfill.

Rnd 16: *Sc in next st, 2 sc in next st; repeat from * around. (27 sc)

Rnd 17: *Sc in next 2 sts, 2 sc in next st.* repeat from * around. (36 sc)

Rnd 18: *Sc in next 3 sts, 2 sc in next st; repeat from * around. (45 sc)

Rnd 19: *Sc in next 4 sts, 2 sc in next st; repeat from * around. (54 sc)

Rnd 20: *Sc next 5 sts, 2 sc in next st; repeat from * around. (63 sc)

Rnd 21: *Sc in next 6 sts, 2 sc in next st; repeat from * around. (72 sc)

Attaching the Eyes

Position the eyes and eye roundies right above the snout, as shown below, and attach them following the instructions under Creating Faces on pages 84–85. Cut the yarn, leaving a 6" tail, draw the yarn through the last stitch to fasten off, weave in tail, and cut off excess yarn.

Rnd 22: *Sc in next 6 sts, sc2tog; repeat from * around. (63 sc)

Rnd 23: *Sc in next 5 sts, sc2tog; repeat from * around. (54 sc)

Rnds 24–25: Sc in each st around. (54 sc)

Rnd 26: *Sc in next 4 sts, sc2tog; repeat from * around. (45 sc)

Rnd 27: *Sc in next 3 sts, sc2tog; repeat from * around. (36 sc)

Rnd 28: *Sc in next 2 sts, sc2tog; repeat from * around. (27 sc)

Stuff with fiberfill almost to the top.

Rnd 29: *Sc in next st, sc2tog; repeat from * around. (18 sc)

Stuff firmly to the top with fiberfill. Insert the precut, predrilled dowel with the screw hole facing out (see pages 88–89). Add more stuffing around the dowel, if necessary, to hold it firmly in place.

Rnd 30: *Sc, skip the next st, sc in the next st; repeat from * around. (12 sc)

Rnd 31: *Sc, skip the next st; repeat from * around. (6 sc)

Slipstitch in first stitch of round, cut yarn, leaving a 6"-long tail, draw the tail through the loop on the hook to fasten off, and weave it in on the wrong side.

Attaching the Ears

Position the ears at an angle as shown below. Use whipstitches to sew the ears in place, draw the yarn through the last stitch to fasten off, and weave in all loose ends. You now have one very cute farm friend.

MOUNTING

See Mounting Your Critter's Head, beginning on page 89, for instructions on how to complete your taxidermy head.

Baaaad Sheep

Finished Measurements

- 11″ wide × 4½″ tall × 6½″ deep

Hook

- US F/5 (3.75 mm) crochet hook

Yarn

- Worsted weight; 1 skein each of black and white (4)

Other Supplies

- Two 12 mm clear plastic animal safety eyes
- Split-ring stitch marker
- Yarn needle
- Fiberfill
- Precut, predrilled dowel: 2″ diameter × 1″ long (see page 91)
- Prepared 11¾″ × 8½″ oval plaque (see page 90)

CROCHETING THE EYE ROUNDIES

(make 2)

Setup: Using the black yarn, ch 2, 6 sc into 2nd chain from hook. Do not pull the tail tight to close hole; leave a small space where you can later insert the eyes. (Place a split-ring stitch marker to mark beginning of each round in the pattern, and move this marker up as you work each round.)

Rnd 1: 2 sc in each st around. (12 sc)

Slipstitch in first stitch of round, cut yarn, leaving a 12"-long tail for later use, and draw the tail through the loop on the hook to fasten off.

CROCHETING THE NOSE ROUNDIES

(make 2)

Setup: Using the black yarn, ch 2, 6 sc into 2nd chain from hook.

Rnd 1: 2 sc in each st around. Pull the tail tight to close hole. (12 sc)

Slipstitch in first stitch of round, cut yarn, leaving a 12"-long tail for later use, and draw the tail through the loop on the hook to fasten off.

CROCHETING THE EARS

(make 2)

Setup: Using the black yarn, ch 2, 6 sc into 2nd chain from hook.

Rnd 1: 2 sc in each st around. Pull tail tight to close hole. (12 sc)

Rnd 2: *1 sc in next st, 2 sc in next st; repeat from * around. (18 sc)

Rnd 3: *Sc in next 2 sts, 2 sc in next st; repeat from * around. (24 sc)

Rnd 4: *Sc in next 3 sts, 2 sc in next st; repeat from * around. (30 sc)

Rnd 5: *Sc in next 4 sts, 2 sc in next st; repeat from * around. (36 sc)

Rnd 6: *Sc in next 5 sts, 2 sc in next st; repeat from * around. (42 sc)

Rnd 7: *Sc in next 6 sts, 2 sc in next st; repeat from * around. (48 sc)

Closing the ear: Slipstitch in first stitch of round, cut yarn, leaving a 12"-long tail for later use, and draw the tail through the loop on the hook to fasten off. Follow the instructions for folded disk ears in A Variety of Ears on page 86 to prepare the ear for attachment later.

CROCHETING THE HEAD

Setup: With the black yarn, ch 2, 6 sc in 2nd chain from hook. (6 sc)

Rnd 1: 2 sc in each ch around. Pull tail tight to close hole. (12 sc)

Rnd 2: *Sc in next st, 2 sc in next st; repeat from * around. (18 sc)

Rnd 3: *Sc in next 2 sts, 2 sc in next st; repeat from * around. (24 sc)

Rnd 4: *Sc in next 3 sts, 2 sc in next st; repeat from * around. (30 sc)

Rnd 5: *Sc in next 4 sts, 2 sc in next st; repeat from * around. (36 sc)

Rnd 6: *Sc in next 5 sts, 2 sc in next st; repeat from * around. (42 sc)

Rnd 7: *Sc in next 6 sts, 2 sc in next st; repeat from * around. (48 sc)

Attaching the Nose Roundies

Position the nose roundies as shown on the facing page, and using matching yarn, whipstitch them securely in place.

Rnds 8–11: *Sc in each st around; repeat from * around. (48 sc)

Rnd 12: *Sc in next 6 sts, sc2tog; repeat from * around. (42 sc)

Rnd 13: *Sc in next 5 sts, sc2tog; repeat from * around. (36 sc)

Rnd 14: *Sc in next 4 sts, sc2tog; repeat from * around. (30 sc)

Rnd 15: *Sc in next 3 sts, sc2tog; repeat from * around. (24 sc)

Rnds 16 and 17: Sc in each st around. (24 sc)

Stuff with fiberfill almost to the top.

Rnd 18: *Sc in next 2 sts, 2 sc in next st; repeat from * around. (32 sc)

Rnd 19: *Sc in next 3 sts, 2 sc in next st; repeat from * around. (40 sc)

Rnds 20–22: Sc in each st around. (40 sc)

Slipstitch in first stitch of round, cut yarn, leaving a 6"-long tail, draw the tail through the loop on the hook to fasten off, and weave it in on the wrong side.

Attaching the Eyes

Position the eye roundies and eyes as shown below right, and follow the instructions under Creating Faces on pages 84–85 to attach them securely to the sheep's head.

Following the instructions for Changing the Yarn Color on page 82, switch to the white yarn.

Rnd 23: *Sc in next 4 sts, 2 sc in next st; repeat from * around. (46 sc)

Rnds 24–26: Sc in each st around. (46 sc)

Rnd 27: *Sc in next 4 sts, sc2tog; repeat from * around. (40 sc)

Rnd 28: *Sc in next 3sts, sc2tog; repeat from * around. (32 sc)

Rnd 29: *Sc in next 2 sts, sc2tog; repeat from * around. (24 sc)

Stuff firmly to the top with fiberfill.

Rnd 30: *Sc in next st, sc2tog; repeat from * around. (16 sc)

Pop in your predrilled, precut dowel with the screw hole facing out (see pages 88–89). Add more stuffing around the dowel, if necessary, to hold it firmly in place.

Rnd 31: *Sc in next st, skip next st; repeat from * around. (10 sc)

Slipstitch in first stitch of round, cut yarn, leaving a 6"-long tail, draw the tail through the loop on the hook to fasten off, and weave it in on the wrong side.

Attaching the Ears

Position the sheep's ears directly above the eyes as shown and whipstitch them securely in place. Draw the yarn through the last stitch to fasten off and weave in the tail.

MOUNTING

See Mounting Your Critter's Head, beginning on page 89, for instructions on how to complete your taxidermy head.

How Now, Brown Cow

Finished Measurements
- 10″ wide × 7″ long × 6″ deep

Hook
- US F/5 (3.75 mm) crochet hook

Yarn
- Worsted weight; 1 skein each of tan, white, and brown

Other Supplies
- Two 18 mm clear plastic animal safety eyes
- Split-ring stitch marker
- Yarn needle
- Fiberfill
- Precut, predrilled dowel: 2″ diameter × 1″ long (see page 91)
- Prepared 9″ × 7″ plaque (see page 90)

CROCHETING THE EYE ROUNDIES
(make 2)

Setup: Using the brown yarn, ch 2, 6 sc in 2nd chain from hook. Don't pull tail tight; leave a small hole where you can later insert the eyes. (Place a split-ring stitch marker to mark beginning of each round in the pattern, and move this marker up as you work each round.)

Rnd 1: 2 sc in each ch around. (12 sc)

Slipstitch in first stitch of round, cut yarn, leaving a 12"-long tail for later use, and draw the tail through the loop on the hook to fasten off.

CROCHETING THE NOSE ROUNDIES
(make 2)

Setup: Using the tan yarn, ch 2, 6 sc in 2nd chain from hook.

Rnd 1: 2 sc in each st around. Pull tail tight to close hole. (12 sc)

Slipstitch in first stitch of round, cut yarn, leaving a 12"-long tail for later use, and draw the tail through the loop on the hook to fasten off.

CROCHETING THE EARS

(make 2)

Setup: Using the brown yarn, ch 2, 6 sc in 2nd chain from hook.

Rnd 1: 2 sc in each st around. Pull tail tight to close hole. (12 sc)

Rnd 2: *Sc in next st, 2 sc in next st; repeat from * around. (18 sc)

Rnd 3: *Sc in next 2 sts, 2 sc in next st; repeat from * around. (24 sc)

Rnd 4: *Sc in next 3 sts, 2 sc in next st; repeat from * around. (30 sc)

Rnd 5: *Sc in next 4 sts, 2 sc in next st; repeat from * around. (36 sc)

Rnd 6: *Sc in next 5 sts, 2 sc in next st; repeat from * around. (42 sc)

Rnd 7: *Sc in next 6 sts, 2 sc in next st; repeat from * around. (48 sc)

Closing the ear: Slipstitch in first stitch of round, cut yarn, leaving a 12"-long tail for later use, and draw the tail through the loop on the hook to fasten off. Follow the instructions for folded disk ears in A Variety of Ears on page 86 to prepare the ear for attachment later.

CROCHETING THE HORNS

(make 2)

Setup: Using the white yarn, ch 2, 6 sc into 2nd chain from hook.

Rnd 1: 2 sc in each st around. Pull tail tight to close hole. (12 sc)

Rnds 2–12: Sc in each st around, stuffing horn along the way.

Following the instructions for Changing the Yarn Color on page 82, switch to the brown yarn.

Rnd 13: Sc in each st around. (12 sc)

Slipstitch in first stitch of round, cut yarn, leaving a 12"-long tail for later use, and draw the tail through the loop on the hook to fasten off.

CROCHETING THE LONG NOSE AND HEAD

Setup: Using the tan yarn, ch 2, 6 sc into 2nd chain from hook.

Rnd 1: 2 sc in each st around. Pull tail tight to close hole. (12 sc)

Rnd 2: *Sc in next st, 2 sc in next st; repeat from * around. (18 sc)

Rnd 3: *Sc in next 2 sts, 2 sc in next st; repeat from * around. (24 sc)

Rnd 4: *Sc in next 3 sts, 2 sc in next st; repeat from * around. (30 sc)

Rnd 5: *Sc in next 4 sts, 2 sc in next st; repeat from * around. (36 sc)

Attaching the Nose Roundies

Position the nose roundies an equal distance apart as shown on the facing page, and using matching yarn, whipstitch them securely in place.

Rnd 6: *Sc in next 4 sts, sc2tog; repeat from * around. (30 sc)

Rnd 7: Sc in each st around. (30 sc)

Switch to the brown yarn.

Rnds 8–11: Sc in each st around. (30 sc)

Rnd 12: *Sc in next 4 sts, sc2tog; repeat from * around. (25 sc)

Rnd 13: Sc in each st around. (25 sc)

Rnd 14: *Sc in next 3 sts, sc2tog; repeat from * around. (20 sc)

Rnd 15: *Sc in each st around. (20 sc)

Stuff almost all the way to the top.

Rnd 16: *Sc in next st, 2 sc next st; repeat from * around. (30 sc)

Rnd 17: *Sc in next 2 sts, 2 sc in next st; repeat from * around. (40 sc)

Rnd 18: *Sc in next 3 sts, 2 sc in next st; repeat from * around. (50 sc)

Rnd 19: *Sc in next 4 sts, 2 sc in next st; repeat from * around. (60 sc)

Rnd 20: *Sc in next 5 sts, 2 sc in next st; repeat from * around. (70 sc)

Rnd 21: *Sc in next 6 sts, 2 sc in next st; repeat from * around. (80 sc)

Attaching the Eyes

Position the eyes and eye roundies as shown on the previous page, and follow the instructions under Creating Faces on pages 84–85 to attach them securely.

Rnd 22: *Sc in next 6 sts, sc2tog; repeat from * around. (70 sc)

Rnd 23: *Sc in next 5 sts, sc2tog; repeat from * around. (60 sc)

Rnds 24–26: Sc in each st around. (60 sc)

Rnd 27: *Sc in next 4 sts, sc2tog; repeat from * around. (50 sc)

Rnd 28: *Sc in next 3 sts, sc2tog; repeat from * around. (40 sc)

Rnd 29: *Sc in next 2sts, sc2tog; repeat from * around. (30 sc)

Stuff with fiberfill almost to the top.

Rnd 30: *Sc in next st, sc2tog; repeat from * around. (20 sc)

Insert your precut, predrilled dowel into the back of the cow's head with the screw hole facing out (see pages 88–89). Add more stuffing around the dowel, if necessary to hold it firmly in place. It's time to close this baby up!

Rnds 31 and 32: *Sc in next st, skip next st; repeat from * around. (5 sc after rnd 32)

Slipstitch in first stitch of round, cut yarn, leaving a 6"-long tail, draw the tail through the loop on the hook to fasten off, and weave it in on the wrong side.

Attaching the Horns

Position the horns on the top of the cow's head right above the eyes as shown on the previous page. Use the long tail to whipstitch the horns to the head, stuffing with additional fiberfill if necessary to make them firm. Draw yarn through last stitch to fasten off and weave in the tail.

Attaching the Ears

Position the ears right in front of the horns as shown, and use matching yarn to stitch them firmly in place. Draw yarn through last stitch to fasten off and weave in the tail.

MOUNTING

See Mounting Your Critter's Head, beginning on page 89, for instructions on how to complete your taxidermy head. Ta-da! You're all done with your Brown Cow!

Dairy Cow

Finished Measurements

- 11″ wide × 5″ long × 6½″ deep

Hook

- US F/5 (3.75 mm) crochet hook

Yarn

- Worsted weight; 1 skein each of black, pale pink, and white (4)

Other Supplies

- Two 18 mm blue plastic animal safety eyes
- Split-ring stitch marker
- Yarn needle
- Fiberfill
- Precut, predrilled dowel: 2″ diameter × 1″ long (see page 91)
- Prepared 9″ × 6¾″ plaque (see page 90)

CROCHETING THE EYE ROUNDIE

(make 1)

Setup: Using the black yarn, ch 2, 6 sc in 2nd chain from hook. Don't pull tail tight; leave a small hole where you can later insert the eye. (Place a split-ring stitch marker to mark beginning of each round in the pattern, and move this marker up as you work each round.)

Rnd 1: 2 sc in each st around. (12 sc)

Rnd 2: Sc, 2 sc in next st. (18 sc)

Slipstitch in first stitch of round, cut yarn, leaving a 12"-long tail for later use, and draw the tail through the loop on the hook to fasten off.

CROCHETING THE NOSE ROUNDIES

(make 2)

Setup: Using the pale pink yarn, ch 2, 6 sc in 2nd chain from hook.

Rnd 1: 2 sc in each st around. Pull tail tight to close hole. (12 sc)

Slipstitch in first stitch of round, cut yarn, leaving a 12"-long tail for later use, and draw the tail through the loop on the hook to fasten off.

CROCHETING THE EARS

(make 2: 1 with the black yarn and 1 with the white yarn)

Setup: Ch 2, 6 sc in 2nd chain from hook.

Rnd 1: 2 sc in each st around. Pull tail tight to close hole. (12 sc)

Rnd 2: *Sc in next st, 2 sc in next st; repeat from * around. (18 sc)

Rnd 3: *Sc in next 2 sts, 2 sc in next st; repeat from * around. (24 sc)

Rnd 4: *Sc in next 3 sts, 2 sc in next st; repeat from * around. (30 sc)

Rnd 5: *Sc in next 4 sts, 2 sc in next st; repeat from * around. (36 sc)

Rnd 6: *Sc in next 5 sts, 2 sc in next st; repeat from * around. (42 sc)

Rnd 7: *Sc in next 6 sts, 2 sc in next st; repeat from * around. (48 sc)

Closing the ear: Slipstitch in first stitch of round, cut yarn, leaving a 12"-long tail for later use, and draw the tail through the loop on the hook to fasten off. Follow the instructions for folded disk ears in A Variety of Ears on page 86 to prepare the ear for attachment later.

CROCHETING THE LONG NOSE AND HEAD

Setup: Using the pale pink yarn, ch 2, 6 sc into 2nd chain from hook.

Rnd 1: 2 sc in each st around. Pull tail tight to close hole. (12 sc)

Rnd 2: *Sc in next st, 2 sc in next st; repeat from * around. (18 sc)

Rnd 3: *Sc in next 2 sts, 2 sc in next st; repeat from * around. (24 sc)

Rnd 4: *Sc in next 3 sts, 2 sc in next st; repeat from * around. (30 sc)

Rnd 5: *Sc in next 4 sts, 2 sc next st; repeat from * around. (36 sc)

Attaching the Nose Roundies

Position the nose roundies on the long nose an equal distance apart as shown on page 137, and using matching yarn, whipstitch them securely in place.

Rnd 6: *Sc in next 4 sts, sc2tog; repeat from * around. (30 sc)

Rnd 7: Sc in each st around. (30 sc)

Following the instructions for Changing the Yarn Color on page 82, switch to the white yarn.

Rnds 8–11: 1 sc in each st around. (30 sc)

Rnd 12: *Sc in next 4 sts, sc2tog; repeat from * around. (24 sc)

Rnd 13: Sc in each st around. (24 sc)

Rnd 14: *Sc in next 3 sts, sc2tog; repeat from * around. (20 sc)

Rnd 15: *Sc in each st around. (20 sc)

Stuff with fiberfill almost to the top.

Rnd 16: *Sc in next st, 2 sc in next st; repeat from * around. (30 sc)

Rnd 17: *Sc in next 2 sts, 2 sc next st; repeat from * around. (40 sc)

Rnd 18: *Sc in next 3 sts, 2 sc in next st; repeat from * around. (50 sc)

Rnd 19: *Sc in next 4 sts, 2 sc in next st; repeat from * around. (60 sc)

Rnd 20: *Sc in next 5 sts, 2 sc in next st; repeat from * around. (70 sc)

Rnd 21 *Sc in next 6 sts, 2 sc in next st; repeat from * around. (80 sc)

Attaching the Eyes

Position the eye and eye roundie on one side of the face, as shown below, and position the other eye directly on the crocheted fabric (no roundie). Follow the instructions under Creating Faces on pages 84–85 to attach all pieces securely.

Rnd 22: *Sc in next 6 sts, sc2tog; repeat from * around. (70 sc)

Rnd 23: *Sc in next 5 sts, sc2tog; repeat from * around. (60 sc)

Rnds 24–26: Sc in each st around. (60 sc)

Rnd 27: *Sc in next 4 sts, sc2tog; repeat from * around. (50 sc)

Rnd 28: *Sc in next 3 sts, sc2tog; repeat from * around. (40 sc)

Rnd 29: *Sc in next 2 sts, sc2tog; repeat from * around. (30 sc)

Stuff with fiberfill almost to the top.

Rnd 30: *Sc into the first sc, sc2tog; repeat from * around. (20 sc)

Insert your precut, predrilled dowel into the back of the cow's head with the screw hole facing out (see pages 88–89). Add more stuffing around the dowel, if necessary, to hold it firmly in place. It's time to close this baby up!

Rnds 31 and 32: *Sc in next st, skip next sc; repeat from * around. (5 sc after rnd 32)

Slipstitch in first stitch of round, cut yarn, leaving a 6"-long tail, draw the tail through the loop on the hook to fasten off, and weave it in on the wrong side.

Attaching the Cow's Ears

Position the ears as shown on the previous page. Thread a yarn needle with matching yarn and whipstitch the ears securely to the head. Draw yarn through last stitch to fasten off and weave in end on the wrong side.

Adding a Topknot

Cut five 6"-long pieces of the white yarn. Locate 5 crochet stitches at the very top of the cow's head. Fold a 6" length of yarn in half and use a crochet hook to draw the folded end through one of the crochet stitches, then draw the cut ends of the yarn through the loop and pull tight to fasten in place (like making fringe on a scarf). Repeat with the remaining lengths of yarn in a circle of crochet stitches to create a little tuft of hair between the cow's ears.

MOUNTING

See Mounting Your Critter's Head, beginning on page 89, for instructions on how to complete your taxidermy head.

Farm Duck

Finished Measurements

- 3″ wide × 3″ long × 7″ deep

Hook

- US F/5 (3.75 mm) crochet hook

Yarn

- Worsted weight; 1 skein each of burnt orange and yellow gold (4)

Other Supplies

- Two 12 mm brown plastic animal safety eyes
- Split-ring stitch marker
- Yarn needle
- Fiberfill
- Precut, predrilled dowel: 1″ diameter × 2″ long (see page 91)
- Prepared 4″ round plaque (see page 90)

CROCHETING THE BILL

Setup: Using the burnt-orange yarn, ch 2, 6 sc into 2nd chain from the hook. (Place a split-ring stitch marker to mark beginning of each round in the pattern, and move this marker up as you work each round.)

Rnd 1: 2 sc in each st around. Pull tail tight to close hole. (12 sc)

Rnds 2–12: Sc in each st around, stuffing with fiberfill as you go. (12 sc)

Following the instructions for Changing the Yarn Color on page 82, switch to the yellow-gold yarn.

Rnd 13: 2 sc in each st around. (24 sc)

Rnds 14–21: Sc in each st around. (24 sc)

Stuff with fiberfill about halfway to the top.

Attaching the Eyes

Position the eyes as shown below, and follow instructions under Creating Faces on pages 84–85 to attach securely.

Rnd 22: *Sc in next 3 sts, sc2tog; repeat from * around. (20 sc)

Rnd 23: *Sc in next 2 sts, sc2tog; repeat from * around. (15 sc)

Rnds 24–31: Sc in each st around, continuing to stuff with fiberfill as you work. (15 sc)

Insert your predrilled and precut dowel into the duck's neck with the screw hole facing out (see pages 88–89). Add more stuffing around the dowel, if necessary, to hold it firmly in place.

Rnd 32: Sc in every other st around. (8 sc)

Slipstitch in first stitch of round, cut yarn, leaving a 6"-long tail, draw the tail through the loop on the hook to fasten off, and weave it in on the wrong side.

MOUNTING

See Mounting Your Critter's Head, beginning on page 89, for instructions on how to complete your taxidermy head.

A Hen and a Rooster

Finished Measurements

- 2½″ wide × 3½″ long × 2¾″ deep

Hook

- US F/5 (3.75 mm) crochet hook

Yarn

- *For the hen:* Worsted weight, 1 skein each of bright yellow, red, and white (4)
- *For the rooster:* Worsted weight, 1 skein each of bright yellow, red, and bright green (4)

Other Supplies

- Four 12mm solid black plastic animal safety eyes
- Split-ring stitch marker
- Yarn needle
- Fiberfill
- Two precut, predrilled dowels: 1″ diameter × 1″ long (see page 91)
- Two prepared 4″ round or square plaques (see page 90)

CROCHETING THE BEAK

Setup: Using the bright yellow yarn, ch 2, 6 sc into 2nd chain from the hook. (Place a splitring stitch marker to mark beginning of each round in the pattern, and move this marker up as you work each round.)

Rnd 1: 2 sc in each st around. Pull tail tight to close hole. (12 sc)

Rnds 2–4: Sc in each st around. (12 sc)

Stuff with fiberfill.

CROCHETING THE HEAD

Following the instructions for Changing the Yarn Color on page 82, switch to the white yarn. (*Note:* The instructions that follow are for the white hen; use the bright green yarn to crochet the rooster. The instructions for the beak, comb, and wattle are the same for both hen and rooster.)

Rnd 1: * Sc in next st, 2 sc in next st; repeat from * around. (18 sc)

Rnd 2: * Sc in next 2 sts, 2 sc in next st; repeat from * around. (24 sc)

Rnd 3: * Sc in next 3 sts, 2 sc in next st; repeat from * around. (30 sc)

Rnds 4–8: Sc in each st around. (30 sc)

Attaching the Eyes

Position the eyes right above the beak as shown on page 143, and follow the instructions under Creating Faces on pages 84–85 to attach them securely.

Rnd 9: * Sc in next 3 sts, sc2tog; repeat from * around. (24 sc)

Rnd 10: * Sc in next 2 sts, sc2tog; repeat from * around. (18 sc)

Rnd 11: * Sc in next st, sc2tog; repeat from * around. (12 sc)

Drop the white yarn, but do not cut it.

CROCHETING THE COMB

This is the fun part! Fold the chicken or rooster head in half, with the fold centered straight between the eyes (see below).

Setup: Insert your hook into the stitch in Round 2 of the white yarn centered between the eyes, and draw through a loop of red yarn. (Leave a short tail of yarn that you can weave back into the head when you've finished crocheting the comb.)

Row 1: Sc in the next 9 sts going from the front to the back of the head, ch 1, turn.

Crocheting the comb

Row 2: Sc in each st, ch 1, turn. (9 sc, not counting the turning chain)

Row 3: Skip the 1st st, * 4 dc in 2nd st, skip the 3rd st, sl st into the 4th st; repeat from * 2 more times. Sl st into the last sc, cut the yarn, leaving a short tail, pull the tail through and weave it into the comb. Weave in the beginning tail and trim excess yarn.

CROCHETING THE WATTLE

Setup: Insert your hook into the stitch in Round 1 of the white yarn centered at the base of the beak, and draw through a loop of red yarn. (Leave a short tail of yarn that you can weave back into the head when you've finished crocheting the wattle.)

Ch 1, 4 dc in next st, sl st in same st. Cut the yarn, leaving a short tail, pull the tail through and weave it into the comb. Weave in the beginning tail and trim excess yarn.

COMPLETING THE HEAD

Stuff the head firmly to the top with fiberfill. Pop in the precut, predrilled dowel with the screw hole facing out (see pages 88–89). Add more stuffing around the dowel, if necessary to hold it firmly in place.

Pick up the white yarn again, and * sc in next st, skip next st; repeat from * around. (8 sc)

Sl st in first stitch of round, cut yarn leaving a short tail, draw the tail through the loop on the hook to fasten off, and weave it in on the wrong side.

MOUNTING

See Mounting Your Critter's Head, beginning on page 89 for instructions on how to complete your taxidermy head.

Cranky Croc

Finished Measurements

- $4\frac{1}{2}$″ wide × $4\frac{1}{2}$″ long × $9\frac{1}{2}$″ deep

Hooks

- US F/5 (3.75 mm) crochet hook
- US E/4 (3.5 mm) crochet hook (for teeth only; see Note at right)

Yarn

- Worsted weight; 1 skein each of olive green and white

- (*Note:* I use cotton for the white yarn, and although it's also graded as yarn weight 4, it's a bit thinner and doesn't fill in as much, so I use a smaller hook for it.)

Other Supplies

- Two 16 mm green plastic reptile or cat safety eyes
- Split-ring stitch marker
- Yarn needle
- Fiberfill
- Precut, predrilled dowel: 2″ diameter × 1″ long (see page 91)
- Prepared 7″ round plaque (see page 90)

CROCHETING THE EYE ROUNDIES

(make 2)

Setup: Using the F/5 (3.75 mm) crochet hook and olive green yarn, ch 2, 6 sc into the 2nd ch from the hook. Don't pull tight; leave a small hole where you can later insert the eyes. (Place a split-ring stitch marker to mark beginning of each round in the pattern, and move this marker up as you work each round.)

Rnd 1: 2 sc in each st around. (12 sc)

Slipstitch in first stitch of round, cut yarn, leaving a 12"-long tail for later use, and draw the tail through the loop on the hook to fasten off.

CROCHETING THE NOSE ROUNDIES

(make 2)

Setup: Using F/5 (3.75 mm) hook and olive green yarn, ch 2, 6 sc in 2nd chain from the hook.

Rnd 1: 2 sc in each st around. Pull tail tight to close hole. (12 sc)

Slipstitch in first stitch of round, cut yarn, leaving a 12"-long tail for later use, and draw the tail through the loop on the hook to fasten off.

CROCHETING THE TEETH

(make 2)

Setup: Using the E/4 (3.5 mm) hook and the white yarn, ch 2, 6 sc in 2nd chain from hook.

Rnd 1: *Sc in next st, 2 sc in next st; repeat from * around. Pull tail tight to close hole. (9 sc)

Rnds 2–5: Sc in each st around. (9 sc)

Following the instructions for Changing the Yarn Color on page 82, switch to the olive green yarn.

Rnd 6: Sc in each st around. Stuff firmly to the top with fiberfill.

Slipstitch in first stitch of round, cut yarn, leaving a 12"-long tail for later use, and draw the tail through the loop on the hook to fasten off.

CROCHETING THE SNOUT AND HEAD

Setup: Using the F/5 (3.75 mm) hook and the olive green yarn, ch 2, 6 sc in 2nd chain from hook.

Rnd 1: 2 sc in each st around. Pull tail tight to close hole. (12 sc)

Rnd 2: *Sc in next st, 2 sc next st; repeat from * around. (18 sc)

Rnd 3: *Sc in next 2 sts, 2 sc in next st; repeat from * around. (24 sc)

Rnd 4: *Sc in next 3 sts, 2 sc in next st; repeat from * around. (30 sc)

Rnd 5: *Sc in next 4 sts, 2 sc in next st; repeat from * around. (36 sc)

Rnds 6 and 7: Sc in each st around. (36 sc)

Attaching the Nose

Position the nose roundies as shown on the next page, and whipstitch them securely in place.

Rnds 8 and 9: Sc in each st around. (36 sc)

Rnd 10: *Sc in next 4 sts, sc2tog; repeat from * around. (30 sc)

Rnd 11: *Sc in next 3 sts, sc2tog; repeat from * around. (24 sc)

Stuff with fiberfill about halfway to the top.

Rnd 12: *Sc in the next 2 sts, sc2tog; repeat from * around. (18 sc)

Stuff firmly to the top with fiberfill.

Rnds 13–18: Sc in each st around, stuffing as you go. (18 sc)

Rnd 19: *Sc in next 8 sts, 2 sc in next st; repeat from * around. (20 sc)

Rnd 20: *Sc in next 9 sts, 2 sc in next st; repeat from * around. (22 sc)

Rnds 21–26: Sc in each st around, stuffing as you go. (22 sc)

Rnd 27: *Sc in next 10 sts, 2 sc in next st; repeat from * around. (24 sc)

Rnds 28–32: Sc in each st around. (24 sc)

Rnd 33: *Sc in next st, 2 sc in next st; repeat from * around. (36 sc)

Rnd 34: *Sc in next 2 sts, 2 sc in next st; repeat from * around. (48 sc)

Rnd 35: *Sc in next 3 sts, 2 sc in next st; repeat from * around. (60 sc)

Rnds 36–42: Sc in each st around.

Attaching the Eyes

Position the eyes and eye roundies just above the base of the snout as shown on the facing page, and follow the instructions under Creating Faces on pages 84–85 to attach them securely.

Rnd 43: *Sc in next 8 sts, sc2tog; repeat from * around. (54 sc)

Rnd 44: *Sc in next 7 sts, sc2tog; repeat from * around. (48 sc)

Rnd 45: *Sc in next 6 sts, sc2tog; repeat from * around. (42 sc)

Rnd 46: *Sc in next 5 sts, sc2tog; repeat from * around. (36 sc)

Rnd 47: *Sc in next 4 sts, sc2tog; repeat from * around. (30 sc)

Rnd 48: *Sc in next 3 sts, sc2tog; repeat from * around. (24 sc)

Stuff firmly to the top with fiberfill. Insert your precut, predrilled dowel into the back of the head with the screw hole facing out (see pages 88–89). Add more stuffing around the dowel, if necessary, to hold it firmly in place.

Rnd 49: *Sc in the next 2 sts, sc2tog; repeat from * around. (18 sc)

Rnd 50: *Sc in the next st, sc2tog; repeat from * around. (12 sc)

Rnd 51: *Sc, skip the next sc; repeat from * around. (8 sc)

Slipstitch in first stitch of round, cut yarn, leaving a 6"-long tail, draw the tail through the loop on the hook to fasten off, and weave it in on the wrong side.

Attaching the Teeth

Position the teeth right below the croc's snout, centered between the nose roundies. Thread a yarn needle with matching yarn and whipstitch the teeth securely to the head, adding more stuffing to firm them up, if needed. Draw yarn through the last stitch to fasten off, and weave in all ends on the wrong side.

MOUNTING

See Mounting Your Critter's Head, beginning on page 89, for instructions on how to complete your taxidermy head.

Flora Flamingo

Finished Measurements

- $2\frac{1}{2}$″ wide × $2\frac{1}{2}$″ long × $7\frac{1}{2}$″ deep

Hook

- US F/5 (3.75 mm) crochet hook

Yarn

- Worsted weight; 1 skein each of black and hot pink (4)

Other Supplies

- Two 12 mm yellow plastic animal safety eyes
- Split-ring stitch marker
- Yarn needle
- Fiberfill
- Precut, predrilled dowel: 1″ diameter × 2″ long (see page 91)
- Prepared 4″ square plaque (see page 90)

CROCHETING THE BILL

Setup: Using the black yarn, ch 2, 6 sc in 2nd chain from hook. (Place a split-ring stitch marker to mark beginning of each round in the pattern, and move this marker up as you work each round.)

Rnd 1: 2 sc in each st around. Pull tail tight to close hole. (12 sc)

Rnds 2–6: Sc in each st around. (12 sc)

Stuff firmly to the top with fiberfill.

Rnd 7: *Sc in next st, 2 sc in next st; repeat from * around. (18 sc)

Rnds 8–13: Sc in each st around. (18 sc)

Rnd 14: *Sc in next st, sc2tog; repeat from * around. (12 sc)

Rnds 15–18: Sc in each st around. (12 sc)

Stuff firmly to the top with fiberfill.

CROCHETING THE BODY

Following the instructions for Changing the Yarn Color on page 82, switch to the hot pink yarn.

Rnd 19: 2 sc in each st around. (24 sc)

Rnds 20–27: Sc in each st around. (24 sc)

Attaching the Eyes

Position the eyes as shown below, and follow the instructions under Creating Faces on pages 84–85 to attach them securely.

Stuff with fiberfill about halfway to the top.

Rnd 28: *Sc in next 4 sts, sc2tog; repeat from * around. (20 sc)

Rnd 29: *Sc in next 2 sts, sc2tog; repeat from * around. (15 sc)

Rnds 30–37: Sc in each st around. (15 sc)

Pop in the precut, predrilled dowel with the screw hole facing out (see pages 88–89). Add more stuffing around the dowel, if necessary, to hold it firmly in place.

Rnd 38: *Sc in next st, skip next st; repeat from * around. (8 sc)

Slipstitch in first stitch of round, cut yarn, leaving a 6" tail, draw the tail through the loop on the hook to fasten off, and weave it in on the wrong side.

MOUNTING

See Mounting Your Critter's Head, beginning on page 89, for instructions on how to complete your taxidermy head.

Krazy Koala

Finished Measurements

- 11″ wide × 6½″ tall × 4″ deep

Hooks

- US F/5 (3.75 mm) crochet hook (for head and ears)
- US D/3 (3.25 mm) crochet hook (for fur around ears)

Yarn

- Worsted weight; 1 skein each of medium gray and black 4
- Super-bulky faux fur; 1 skein of silver gray 6

Other Supplies

- Two 18 mm clear plastic animal safety eyes
- Split-ring stitch marker
- Yarn needle
- Fiberfill
- Precut, predrilled dowel: 2″ diameter × 1″ long (see page 91)
- Prepared 11½″ × 8½″ plaque (see page 90)

If you wish to give your koala a sleepy look, cut two 12" pieces of the medium gray worsted-weight yarn, and set aside for creating the sleepy eyelids later in the pattern.

CROCHETING THE EYE ROUNDIES

(make 2)

Setup: Using the medium gray yarn, ch 2, 6 sc in 2nd chain from hook. Don't pull tail tight; leave a small hole where you can later insert the eye. (Place a split-ring stitch marker to mark beginning of each round in the pattern, and move this marker up as you work each round.)

Rnd 1: 2 sc in each st around. (12 sc)

Slipstitch in first stitch of round, cut yarn, leaving a 12"-long tail for later use, and draw the tail through the loop on the hook to fasten off.

CROCHETING THE EARS

(make 4)

Setup: Using the medium gray yarn and the F/5 (3.75 mm) hook, ch 2, 6 sc in 2nd chain from hook.

Rnd 1: 2 sc in each st around. Pull tail tight to close hole. (12 sc)

Rnd 2: *Sc in next st, 2 sc in next st; repeat from * around. (18 sc)

Rnd 3: *Sc in next 2 sts, 2 sc in next st; repeat from * around. (24 sc)

Rnd 4: *Sc in next 3 sts, 2 sc in next st; repeat from * around. (30 sc)

Rnd 5: *Sc in next 4 sts, 2 sc in next st; repeat from * around. (36 sc)

Rnd 6: *Sc in next 5 sts, 2 sc in next st; repeat from * around. (42 sc)

Rnd 7: *Sc in next 6 sts, 2 sc in next st; repeat from * around. (48 sc)

Slipstitch in first stitch of round, cut yarn, leaving an extra-long tail for later use, and draw it through loop to fasten off.

Make three more ears: one with an extra-long tail and the other two with shorter 6"-long tails. Weave in the short tails before proceeding to the next step.

Position one of the ears with a 12"-long tail on top of one with a 6"-long tail with their wrong sides facing each other. Using matching yarn, whipstitch around the entire edge to join the two ear pieces. Draw the tail through the last stitch to fasten off, and leave the tail for later use. Repeat with the two remaining ears. (See A Variety of Ears on page 86 for an illustration of how to do this.)

ADDING THE FUZZY TUFTS TO THE EARS

Rnd 1: Using the silver gray faux fur yarn and the D/3 (3.25 mm) hook, sc in each st around five sides of the ear, fluffing the yarn as you work. (Leave the sixth side unedged; this is the side that will later be sewn onto the head.)

Slipstitch in last st on fifth side of the ear, cut yarn, leaving a 6"-long tail, draw it through loop to fasten off, and weave it in on the wrong side. Fluff the ear fuzz more if necessary. It's okay if a few fur hairs come loose and fall out — it happens. Weave in beginning tail as well. Repeat for second ear. (For tips on working with novelty yarns, see Here Comes the Fuzz, page 88.)

CROCHETING THE NOSE

Setup: Using the black yarn and the F/5 (3.75 mm) hook, ch 2, 6 sc in 2nd chain from hook.

Rnd 1: 2 sc in each st around. Pull tail tight to close hole. (12 sc)

Rnd 2: *Sc in next st, 2 sc in next st; repeat from * around. (18 sc)

Rnds 3–5: Sc in each st around. (18 sc)

Following the instructions for Changing the Yarn Color on page 82, switch to the medium gray yarn.

Rnd 6: Sc in each st around. (18 sc)

Slipstitch in first stitch of round, cut yarn, leaving a 12"-long tail for later use, and draw the tail through the loop on the hook to fasten off. Stuff firmly to the top with fiberfill.

CROCHETING THE HEAD

Setup: Using the medium gray yarn and F/5 (3.75 mm) hook, ch 2, 6 sc in 2nd chain from hook.

Rnd 1: 2 sc in each st around. Pull tail tight to close hole. (12 sc)

Rnd 2: *Sc in next st, 2 sc in next st; repeat from * around. (18 sc)

Rnd 3: *Sc in next 2 sts, 2 sc in next st; repeat from * around. (24 sc)

Rnd 4: *Sc in next 3 sts, 2 sc in next st; repeat from * around. (30 sc)

Rnd 5: *Sc in next 4 sts, 2 sc in next st; repeat from * around. (36 sc)

Rnd 6: *Sc in next 5 sts, 2 sc in next st; repeat from * around. (42 sc)

Rnd 7: *Sc in next 6 sts, 2 sc in next st; repeat from * around. (48 sc)

Rnd 8: *Sc in next 7 sts, 2 sc in next st; repeat from * around. (54 sc)

Rnd 9: *Sc in next 8 sts, 2 sc in next st; repeat from * around. (60 sc)

Rnd 10: *Sc in next 9 sts, 2 sc in next st; repeat from * around. (66 sc)

Attaching the Nose

Position the nose in the center of the face, shaping it into an oval and orienting it vertically so that it resembles a typical koala bear nose, as shown on the facing page. Thread a yarn needle with matching yarn, and whipstitch all the way around the edge to attach securely. Draw the yarn through the last stitch to fasten off and weave in end on wrong side.

Attaching the Eyes and Eye Roundies

Position the eyes and eye roundies as shown, and follow the instructions under Creating Faces on pages 84–85 to attach them securely. If you wish to give your koala a sleepy look, see page 87 for the Sleepy-Eye technique.

Rnd 11: *Sc in next 9 sts, 2sctog; repeat from * around. (60 sc)

Rnd 12: *Sc in next 8 sts, sc2tog; repeat from * around. (54 sc)

Rnds 13 and 14: 1 sc in each st around; repeat from * around. (54 sc)

Rnd 15: *Sc in next 7 sts, sc2tog; repeat from * around. (48 sc)

Rnd 16: *Sc in next 6 sts, sc2tog; repeat from * around. (42 sc)

Rnd 17: *Sc in next 5 sts, sc2tog; repeat from * around. (36 sc)

Rnd 18: *Sc in next 4 sts, sc2tog; repeat from * around. (30 sc)

Stuff with fiberfill about halfway to the top.

Rnd 19: *Sc in next 3 sts, sc2tog; repeat from * around. (24 sc)

Stuff firmly to the top with fiberfill. Pop in the precut, predrilled dowel with the screw hole facing out (see pages 88–89). Add more stuffing around the dowel, if necessary, to hold it firmly in place.

Rnd 20: *Sc in next 2 sts, sc2tog; repeat from * around. (18 sc)

Rnd 21: *Sc in next st, sc2tog; repeat from * around. (12 sc)

Rnd 22: *Sc in next st, skip next st; repeat from * around. (8 sc)

Slipstitch in first stitch of round, cut yarn, leaving a 6"-long tail, draw the tail through the loop on the hook to fasten off, and weave it in on the wrong side.

Attaching the Ears

Position the ears on opposite sides of the head, right next to the eyes as shown. For a perky, alert expression, position the ears high on the head and a bit toward the center. Thread a yarn needle with matching yarn and whipstitch along the untrimmed edge of the ears to attach them securely. Draw the yarn through the last stitch to fasten off and weave in the tail on the wrong side. Refluff the fuzz, if needed.

MOUNTING

See Mounting Your Critter's Head, beginning on page 89, for instructions on how to complete your taxidermy head.

Panda Bear

Finished Measurements

- 7″ wide × 6″ long × 4½″ deep

Hook

- US F/5 (3.75 mm) crochet hook

Yarn

- *For Panda Bear:* Worsted weight; 1 skein each of black and white
- *For Polar Bear (page 159):* 1 skein of white (4)

Other Supplies

- *For Panda Bear:* One 22 mm black plastic animal safety nose
- *For Polar Bear:* One 20 mm textured black plastic animal safety nose
- *For both bears:* Two 12 mm clear plastic animal safety eyes
- Split-ring stitch marker
- Yarn needle
- Fiberfill
- Precut, predrilled dowel: 2″ diameter × 1″ long (see page 91)
- Prepared 7″ square or round plaque (see page 90)

Note: The instructions that follow are for the panda bear; for the polar bear, use all white yarn.

CROCHETING THE EYE ROUNDIES

(make 2)

Setup: Using the black yarn, ch 2, 6 sc into 2nd chain from the hook. Don't pull tail tight; leave a small hole where you can later insert the eyes. (Place a split-ring stitch marker to mark beginning of each round in the pattern, and move this marker up as you work each round.)

Rnd 1: 2 sc in each st around. (12 sc)

Slipstitch in first stitch of round, cut

yarn, leaving a 12"-long tail for later use, and draw the tail through the loop on the hook to fasten off.

CROCHETING THE EARS

(make 2)

Setup: Using the black yarn, ch 2, 6 sc into 2nd chain from hook.

Rnd 1: 2 sc in each st around. Pull tail tight to close hole. (12 sc)

Rnd 2: *Sc in next st, 2 sc in next st; repeat from * around. (18 sc)

Rnds 3–5: Sc in each st around. (18 sc)

Rnd 6: *Sc in next 7 sts, sc2tog; repeat from * around. (16 sc)

Rnd 7: Sc in each st around. (16 sc)

Closing the ear: Slipstitch in first stitch of round, cut yarn, leaving a 12"-long tail for later use, and draw the tail through the loop on the hook to fasten off. Flatten the tube and use the long tail to sew the opening closed. (See an illustration for the tube ear on page 86 in A Variety of Ears for an illustration of how to do this.)

CROCHETING THE NOSE AND HEAD

Setup: Using the white yarn, ch 2, 6 sc into 2nd chain from hook. Don't pull tail tight; leave a small hole where you can later insert the plastic nose.

Rnd 1: 2 sc in each st around. (12 sc)

Rnd 2: *Sc in next st, 2 sc in next st; repeat from * around. (18 sc)

Rnds 3–8: Sc in each st around. (18 sc)

Attaching the Nose

Position the nose as shown on the next page, and follow the instructions under Creating Faces on pages 84–85 to attach it securely.

Stuff firmly to the top with fiberfill.

Rnd 9: *Sc in next st, 2 sc in next st; repeat from * around. (27 sc)

Rnd 10: *Sc in next 2 sts, 2 sc in next st; repeat from * around. (36 sc)

Rnd 11: *Sc in next 3 sts, 2 sc in next st; repeat from * around. (45 sc)

Rnd 12: *Sc in next 4 sts, 2 sc in next st; repeat from * around. (54 sc)

Rnd 13: *Sc in next 5 sts, 2 sc in next st; repeat from * around. (63 sc)

Rnd 14: *Sc in next 6 sts, 2 sc in next st; repeat from * around. (72 sc)

Attaching the Eyes and Eye Roundies

Position the eyes and eye roundies just above the nose as shown on the next page, and follow the instructions under Creating Faces (page 85) to attach them securely.

Rnd 15: *Sc in next 6 sts, sc2tog; repeat from * around. (63 sc)

Rnd 16: *Sc in next 5 sts, sc2tog; repeat from * around. (54 sc)

Rnds 17 and 18: Sc in each st around. (54 sc)

Rnd 19: *Sc in next 4 sts, sc2tog; repeat from * around. (45 sc)

Rnd 20: *Sc in next 3 sts, sc2tog; repeat from * around. (36 sc)

Stuff with fiberfill about halfway to the top.

Rnd 21: *Sc in next 2 sts, sc2tog; repeat from * around. (27 sc)

Rnd 22: *Sc in next st, sc2tog; repeat from * around. (18 sc)

Stuff firmly to the top with fiberfill. Pop in the precut, predrilled dowel with the screw hole facing out (see pages 88–89). Add more stuffing around the dowel, if necessary, to hold it firmly in place.

Rnd 23: *Sc in next st, skip the next st; repeat from * around. (12 sc)

Slipstitch in first stitch of round, cut yarn, leaving a 6"-long tail, draw the tail through the loop on the hook to fasten off, and weave it in on the wrong side.

Attaching the Ears

For a perky, alert expression, position the ears about 3 rounds back and just above the eye roundies, as shown below. Use whipstitches to attach them securely, and draw yarn through the last stitch to fasten off. Weave in any loose ends.

MOUNTING

See Mounting Your Critter's Head, beginning on page 89, for instructions on how to complete your taxidermy head.

Timid Toucan

Finished Measurements
- 3½″ wide × 3½″ long × 6½″ deep

Hook
- US F/5 (3.75 mm) crochet hook

Yarn
- Worsted weight; 1 skein each of black, yellow-green, turquoise, and white

Other Supplies
- Two 18 mm blue plastic animal safety eyes
- Split-ring stitch marker
- Yarn needle
- Fiberfill
- Precut, predrilled dowel: 2″ diameter × 1″ long (see page 91)
- Prepared 5″ square plaque (see page 90)

CROCHETING THE EYE ROUNDIES
(make 2)

Setup: Using the white yarn, ch 2, 6 sc in 2nd chain from hook. Don't pull tail tight; leave a small hole where you can later insert the eye. (Place a split-ring stitch marker to mark beginning of each round in the pattern, and move this marker up as you work each round.)

Rnd 1: 2 sc in each st around. (12 sc)

Rnd 2: *Sc in next st, 2 sc in next st; repeat from * around. (18 sc)

Slipstitch in first stitch of round, cut yarn, leaving a 12"-long tail for later use, and draw the tail through the loop on the hook to fasten off.

CROCHETING THE BEAK
Setup: Using the black yarn, ch 2, 6 sc in 2nd chain from hook.

Rnd 1: 2 sc in each st around. Pull tail tight to close hole. (12 sc)

Rnds 2–4: Sc in each st around. (12 sc)

Rnd 5: *Sc in next st, 2 sc in next st; repeat from * around. (18 sc)

Rnds 6 and 7: Sc in each st around.

Following the instructions under Changing the Yarn Color on page 82, switch to the yellow-green yarn.

Rnd 8: *Sc in next 2 sts, 2 sc in the next st; repeat from * around. (24 sc)

Rnd 9: *Sc in next 3 sts, 2 sc in next st; repeat from * around. (30 sc)

Rnds 10–12: Sc in each st around. (30 sc)

Rnd 13: *Sc in next 3 sts, sc2tog; repeat from * around. (24 sc)

Stuff firmly to the top with fiberfill.

Switch to the turquoise yarn.

Rnd 14: *Sc in next 2 sts, sc2tog; repeat from * around. (18 sc)

Rnds 15–18: Sc in each st around. (18 sc)

Switch to the black yarn.

Rnd 19: *Sc in next st, 2 sc in the next st; repeat from * around. (27 sc)

Rnd 20: Sc in each st around. (27 sc)

Rnd 21: *Sc in next 2 sts, 2 sc in next st; repeat from * around. (36 sc)

Rnds 22–28: Sc in each st around. (36 sc)

Attaching the Eyes and Eye Roundies

Position the eyes and eye roundies as shown below, and follow the instructions under Creating Faces on pages 84–85 to attach them securely.

Stuff with fiberfill about halfway to the top.

Rnd 29: *Sc in next 4 sts, sc2tog; repeat from * around. (30 sc)

Rnd 30: *Sc in next 3 sts, sc2tog; repeat from * around. (24 sc)

Pop the precut, predrilled dowel rod into the back of the head with the screw hole facing out (see pages 88–89). Add more fiberfill around the dowel, if necessary, to hold it firmly in place.

Rnd 31: *Sc in next 2 sts, sc2tog; repeat from * around. (18 sc)

Rnd 32: *Sc in next st, sc2tog; repeat from * around. (12 sc)

Slipstitch in first stitch of round, cut yarn, leaving a 6"-long tail. Draw the tail through the loop on the hook to fasten off, and weave it in on the wrong side.

Now for the finishing touch! Cut one 6" length each of the black, yellow-green, and turquoise yarns. Loop each piece through the top of the head, like adding fringe to a scarf, as shown above. You can add more lengths of each color if you'd like to make the tuft of feathers thicker. There you go — you have one very colorful toucan!

MOUNTING

See Mounting Your Critter's Head, beginning on page 89, for instructions on how to complete your taxidermy head.

Ellie the Elephant

Finished Measurements

- 9″ wide × 5″ long × 6¼″ deep

Hook

- US F/5 (3.75 mm) crochet hook

Yarn

- Worsted weight; 1 skein each of lilac and white (4)

Other Supplies

- Two 12 mm clear plastic animal safety eyes
- Split-ring stitch marker
- Yarn needle
- Fiberfill
- Precut, predrilled dowel: 2″ diameter × 1″ long (see page 91)
- Prepared 9″ × 7″ plaque (see page 90)

Abbreviations

- **sc tbl** Single crochet through back loop only (see page 201)

CROCHETING THE EYE ROUNDIES

(make 2)

Setup: Using the lilac yarn, ch 2, 6 sc into 2nd chain from hook. Don't pull tail tight; leave a small hole where you can later insert the eyes. (Place a split-ring stitch marker to mark beginning of each round in the pattern, and move this marker up as you work each round.)

Rnd 1: 2 sc in each st around. (12 sc)

Rnd 2: *Sc in next st, 2 sc in next st; repeat from * around. (18 sc)

Slipstitch in first stitch of round, cut yarn, leaving a 12"-long tail for later use, and draw the tail through the loop on the hook to fasten off.

CROCHETING THE EARS

(make 2)

Setup: Using the lilac yarn, ch 2, 6 sc into 2nd chain from the hook.

Rnd 1: 2 sc in each st around. Pull tail tight to close hole. (12 sc)

Rnd 2: *Sc in next st, 2 sc in next st; repeat from * around. (18 sc)

Rnd 3: *Sc in next st, 2 sc in next st; repeat from * around. (24 sc)

Rnd 4: *Sc in next 3 sts, 2 sc in next st; repeat from * around. (30 sc)

Rnd 5: *Sc in next 4 sts, 2 sc in next st; repeat from * around. (36 sc)

Rnd 6: *Sc in next 5 sts, 2 sc in next st; repeat from * around. (42 sc)

Rnd 7: *Sc in next 6 sts, 2 sc in next st; repeat from * around. (48 sc)

Rnd 8: *Sc in next 7 sts, 2 sc in next st; repeat from * around. (54 sc)

Rnd 9: *Sc in next 8 sts, 2 sc in next st; repeat from * around. (60 sc)

Closing the ear: Slipstitch in first stitch of round, cut yarn, leaving a 20"-long tail for later use, and draw the tail through the loop on the hook to fasten off. Fold the ear in half with the points of the hexagon aligned, and whipstitch all the way around the edge. (See A Variety of Ears on page 86 for an illustration of how to do this.)

CROCHETING THE TUSKS

(make 2)

Setup: Using the white yarn, ch 2, 6 sc into 2nd chain from hook.

Rnd 1: 2 sc in each st around. Pull tail tight to close hole. (12 sc)

Rnds 2–8: Sc in each st around. (12 sc)

Rnd 9: Following the instructions under Changing the Yarn Color on page 82, switch to the lilac yarn, and sc in each st around. (12 sc)

Slipstitch in last stitch, cut yarn, leaving a 12"-long tail, draw tail through last stitch to fasten off, and leave tail for later use.

Stuff firmly to the top with fiberfill.

CROCHETING THE TRUNK

Setup: Using the lilac yarn, ch 2, 6 sc into 2nd chain from hook.

Rnd 1: 2 sc in each st around. Pull tail tight to close hole. (12 sc)

Rnd 2: *Sc in next st, 2 sc in next st; repeat from * around. (18 sc)

Rnd 3: *Sc in next 2 sts, 2 sc in next st; repeat from * around. (24 sc)

Rnd 4: Sc tbl in each st around. (24 sc)

Rnds 5 and 6: Sc tbl in each st around. (24 sc)

Stuff with fiberfill as you work.

Rnd 7: *Sc in next 6 sts, sc2tog; repeat from * around. (20 sc)

Rnd 8: Sc in each st around. (20 sc)

Rnd 9: *Sc in next 5 sts, sc2tog; repeat from * around. (18 sc)

Rnd 10: 1 sc in each st around. (18 sc)

Rnd 11: *Sc in next 4 sts, sc2tog; repeat from * around. (15 sc)

Rnd 12: Sc in each st around. (15 sc)

Rnd 13: *Sc in next 3 sts, sc2tog; repeat from * around. (12 sc)

Rnd 14: Sc in each st around. (12 sc)

Stuff firmly to the top with fiberfill.

FORMING THE HEAD

Rnd 15: *Sc in next st, 2 sc in next st; repeat from * around. (18 sc)

Rnd 16: *Sc in next 2 sts, 2 sc in next st; repeat from * around. (24 sc)

Rnd 17: *Sc in next 3 sts, 2 sc in next st; repeat from * around. (30 sc)

Rnd 18: *Sc in next 4 sts, 2 sc in next st; repeat from * around. (36 sc)

Rnd 19: *Sc in next 5 sts, 2 sc in next st; repeat from * around. (42 sc)

Rnd 20: *Sc in next 6 sts, 2 sc in next st; repeat from * around. (48 sc)

Rnd 21: *Sc in next 7 sts, 2 sc in next st; repeat from * around. (54 sc)

Rnd 22: *Sc in next 8 sts, 2 sc in next st; repeat from * around. (60 sc)

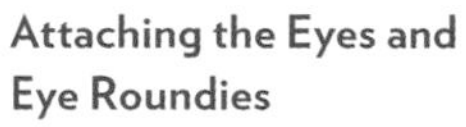

Attaching the Eyes and Eye Roundies

Position the eyes and eye roundies as shown below left, and follow the instructions under Creating Faces on pages 84–85 to attach them securely.

Rnds 23–25: Sc in each st around. (60 sc)

Rnd 26: *Sc in next 8 sts, sc2tog; repeat from * around. (54 sc)

Rnd 27: *Sc in next 7 sts, sc2tog; repeat from * around. (48 sc)

Rnd 28: *Sc in next 6 sts, sc2tog; repeat from * around. (42 sc)

Rnd 29: *Sc in next 5 sts, sc2tog; repeat from * around. (36 sc)

Rnd 30: *Sc in next 4 sts, sc2tog; repeat from * around. (30 sc)

Stuff almost to the top with fiberfill.

Rnd 31: *Sc in next 3 sts, sc2tog; repeat from * around. (24 sc)

Rnd 32: *Sc in next 2 sts, sc2tog; repeat from * around. (18 sc)

Stuff firmly to the top with fiberfill. Pop in your precut, predrilled dowel with the the screw hole facing out (see pages 88–89). Add more stuffing around the dowel, if necessary, to hold it firmly in place. It's time to close her up!

Rnd 33: *Sc in next st, sc2tog; repeat from * around. (12 sc)

Rnd 34: *Sc, skip next st; repeat from * around. (8 sc)

Slipstitch in first stitch of round, cut yarn, leaving a 6"-long tail, draw the tail through the loop on the hook to fasten off, and weave it in on the wrong side.

Attaching the Tusks

Position one tusk right below an eye roundie, next to the trunk as shown on the previous page. Thread a yarn needle with matching yarn, and use whipstitches to sew the tusk securely in place. Draw yarn through last stitch to fasten off, cut yarn, and weave in tail on the wrong side. Repeat for the other tusk, making sure it's symmetrical with the first.

Attaching the Ears

Position the ears as shown on the previous page, with the folded edge against the head. You are going to attach the center 2" of each ear to the head. Make sure the ears are at the same level and an equal distance from the center of the face. You'll have to eyeball this to get it right. Thread a yarn needle with matching yarn, and use whipstitches to sew each ear securely in place. Draw yarn through last stitch to fasten off, cut yarn, and weave in tail on the wrong side.

MOUNTING

See Mounting Your Critter's Head, beginning on page 89, for instructions on how to complete your taxidermy head.

Graceful Giraffe

Finished Measurements

- 8½″ wide × 7½″ long × 6¼″ deep

Hook

- US F/5 (3.75 mm) crochet hook

Yarn

- Worsted weight; 1 skein each of yellow and brown

Other Supplies

- Two 12 mm clear plastic animal safety eyes
- Split-ring stitch marker
- Yarn needle
- Fiberfill
- Precut, predrilled dowel: 2″ diameter × 1″ long (see page 91)
- Prepared 9″ × 7″ shield-style plaque (see page 90)

CROCHETING THE EYE ROUNDIES

(make 2)

Setup: Using the yellow yarn, ch 2, 6 sc in 2nd chain from hook. Don't pull tail tight; leave a small hole where you can later insert the eyes. (Place a split-ring stitch marker to mark beginning of each round in the pattern and move this marker up as you work each round.)

Rnd 1: 2 sc in each st around. (12 sc)

Slipstitch in first stitch of round, cut yarn, leaving a 12"-long tail for later use, and draw the tail through the loop on the hook to fasten off.

CROCHETING THE NOSE ROUNDIES

(make 2)

Setup: Using the brown yarn, ch 2, 6 sc in 2nd chain from hook.

Rnd 1: 2 sc in each st around. Pull tail tight to close hole. (12 sc)

Slipstitch in first stitch of round, cut yarn, leaving a 12"-long tail for later use, and draw the tail through the loop on the hook to fasten off.

CROCHETING THE EARS

(make 2)

Setup: Using the yellow yarn, ch 2, 6 sc in 2nd chain from hook.

Rnd 1: 2 sc in each st around. Pull tail tight to close hole. (12 sc)

Rnd 2: *Sc in next st, 2 sc in next st; repeat from * around. (18 sc)

Rnd 3: *Sc in next 2 sts, 2 sc in next st; repeat from * around. (24 sc)

Rnd 4: *Sc in next 3 sts, 2 sc in next st; repeat from * around. (30 sc)

Rnd 5: *Sc in next 4 sts, 2 sc in next st; repeat from * around. (36 sc)

Closing the ear: Slipstitch in first stitch of round, cut yarn, leaving a 12"-long tail for later use, and draw the tail through the loop on the hook to fasten off. Follow the instructions for the folded disk ear in A Variety of Ears on page 86 to prepare the ear for attachment later.

CROCHETING THE HORN NUBS

(make 2)

Setup: Using the brown yarn, ch 2, 6 sc into the 2nd chain from hook.

Rnd 1: 2 sc in each st around. Pull tail tight to close hole. (12 sc)

Rnd 2: *Sc in next st, 2 sc in next st; repeat from * around. (18 sc)

Rnd 3: *Sc in next 2 sts, 2 sc in next st; repeat from * around. (24 sc)

Rnds 4–8: Sc in each st around. (24 sc)

Rnd 9: *Sc in next 2 sts, sc2tog; repeat from * around. (18 sc)

Stuff with fiberfill about halfway to the top.

Rnd 10: *Sc in next st, sc2tog; repeat from * around. (12 sc)

Following the instructions for Changing the Yarn Color on page 82, switch to the yellow yarn.

Rnds 11–14: Sc in each st around. (12 sc)

Slipstitch in the last sc, pulling through a 12"-long tail of yarn to use to later sew the nub onto the head. Stuff all the way. Set aside.

CROCHETING THE NOSE AND HEAD

Setup: Using the brown yarn, ch 2, 6 sc into 2nd chain from hook.

Rnd 1: 2 sc in each st around. Pull tail tight to close hole. (12 sc)

Rnd 2: *Sc in next st, 2 sc in next st; repeat from * around. (18 sc)

Rnd 3: *Sc in next 2 sts, 2 sc in next st; repeat from * around. (24 sc)

Rnd 4: *Sc in next 3 sts, 2 sc in next st; repeat from * around. (30 sc)

Rnd 5: *Sc in next 4 sts, 2 sc in next st; repeat from * around. (36 sc)

Attaching the Nose Roundies

Position nose roundies an equal distance apart as shown on the facing page. Thread a yarn needle with matching yarn, and use whipstitches to sew the roundies securely in place. Draw yarn through last stitch to fasten off, and weave in tail on the wrong side.

Rnd 6: *Sc in next 4 sts, sc2tog; repeat from * around. (30 sc)

Rnd 7: *Sc in each st around. (30 sc)

Switch to the yellow yarn.

Rnds 8–11: Sc in each st around. (30 sc)

Rnd 12: *Sc in next 4 sts, sc2tog; repeat from * around. (24 sc)

Rnd 13: Sc in each st around. (24 sc)

Rnd 14: *Sc in next 3 sts, sc2tog; repeat from * around. (20 sc)

Rnd 15: Sc in each st around. (20 sc)

Stuff almost all the way to the top.

Rnd 16: *Sc in next st, 2 sc in next st; repeat from * around. (30 sc)

Rnd 17: *Sc in next 2 sts, 2 sc in next st; repeat from * around. (40 sc)

Rnd 18: *Sc in next 3 sts, 2 sc in next st; repeat from * around. (50 sc)

Rnd 19: *Sc in next 4 sts, 2 sc in next st; repeat from * around. (60 sc)

Rnd 20: *Sc in next 5 sts, 2 sc in next st; repeat from * around. (70 sc)

Rnd 21: *Sc in next 6 sts, 2 sc in next st; repeat from * around. (80 sc)

Attaching the Eyes and Eye Roundies

Position the eyes and eye roundies as shown at left, and follow the instructions under Creating Faces on pages 84–85 to attach them securely.

Rnd 22: *Sc in next 6 sts, sc2tog; repeat from * around. (70 sc)

Rnd 23: *Sc in next 5 sts, sc2tog; repeat from * around. (60 sc)

Rnds 24–26: Sc in each st around. (60 sc)

Rnd 27: *Sc in next 4 sts, sc2tog; repeat from * around. (50 sc)

Rnd 28: *Sc in next 3 sts, sc2tog; repeat from * around. (40 sc)

Rnd 29: *Sc in next 2 sts, sc2tog; repeat from * around. (30 sc)

Stuff with fiberfill almost to the top.

Rnd 30: *Sc in next st, sc2tog; repeat from * around. (20 sc)

Place your precut, predrilled dowel into the back of the head with the screw hole facing out (see pages 88–89). Add more stuffing around the dowel, if necessary, to hold it firmly in place. Let's close her up!

Rnds 31 and 32: *Sc in next st, skip the next st; repeat from * around. (6 sc)

Slipstitch in first stitch of round, cut yarn, leaving a 6"-long tail, draw the tail through the loop on the hook to fasten off, and weave it in on the wrong side.

Attaching the Nubs

Position the nubs on the top of the head right above the eyes as shown on the previous page. Thread the saved long tail through a yarn needle and use whipstitches to sew each of the nubs securely in place. Add extra stuffing to make the nubs stiff, if necessary. Draw the yarn through the last stitch to fasten off and weave in tail on the wrong side.

Attaching the Ears

Position the ears right in front of the nubs as shown. Thread a yarn needle with matching yarn and use whipstitches to sew the ears securely in place. Draw the yarn through the last stitch to fasten off and weave tails to the wrong side.

MOUNTING

See Mounting Your Critter's Head, beginning on page 89, for instructions on how to complete your taxidermy head. Now you have yourself a cute giraffe.

Hipster Hippo

Finished Measurements
- 4″ wide × 5½″ deep × 5½″ tall

Hook
- US F/5 (3.75 mm) crochet hook

Yarn
- Worsted weight; 1 skein gray or light green and 1 skein of white (4)

Other Supplies
- Two 12 mm clear plastic animal safety eyes
- Split-ring stitch marker
- Yarn needle
- Fiberfill
- Precut, predrilled dowel: 2″ diameter × 1″ long (see page 91)
- Prepared 7″ round plaque (see page 90)

Abbreviations
- **sc tfl** Single crochet through front loop only (see page 201)

Note: The instructions on the following pages are for the gray hippo; change to light green if you prefer.

CROCHETING THE EYE ROUNDIES

(make 2)

Setup: Using the gray yarn, ch 2, 6 sc into the 2nd ch from the hook. Don't pull tight; leave a small hole where you can later insert the eyes. (Place a split-ring stitch marker to mark beginning of each round in the pattern, and move this marker up as you work each round.)

Rnd 1: 2 sc in each st around. (12 sc)

Slipstitch in first stitch of round, cut yarn, leaving a 12"-long tail for later use, and draw the tail through the loop on the hook to fasten off.

CROCHETING THE NOSE ROUNDIES

(make 2)

Setup: Using the gray yarn, ch 2, 6 sc in 2nd chain from the hook.

Rnd 1: 2 sc in each st around. Pull tail tight to close hole. (12 sc)

Slipstitch in first stitch of round, cut yarn, leaving a 12"-long tail for later use, and draw the tail through the loop on the hook to fasten off.

CROCHETING THE TEETH

(make 2)

Setup: Using the white yarn, ch 2, 6 sc in the 2nd chain from hook.

Rnd 1: 2 sc in each st around. Pull tail tight to close hole. (12 sc)

Rnd 2: Sc tfl in each st around. (12 sc)

Rnds 3–4: Sc in each st around. Stuff with fiberfill. (12 sc)

Following the instructions for Changing the Yarn Color on page 82, switch to the gray yarn.

Rnd 5: Sc in each st around. (12 sc)

Slipstitch in first stitch of round, cut yarn, leaving a 12"-long tail for later use, and draw the tail through the loop on the hook to fasten off. Weave all ends in securely on the wrong side.

CROCHETING THE EARS

(make 2)

Setup: Using the gray yarn, ch 2, 6 sc in 2nd chain from hook.

Rnd 1: 2 sc in each st around. Pull tail tight to close hole. (12 sc)

Rnd 2: *Sc in next st, 2 sc in next st; repeat from * around. (18 sc)

Rnd 3: *Sc in next 2 sts, 2 sc in next st; repeat from * around. (24 sc)

Rnd 4: *Sc in next 3 sts, 2 sc in next st; repeat from * around. (30 sc)

Closing the ear: Slipstitch in first stitch of round, cut yarn, leaving a 12"-long tail for later use, and draw the tail through the loop on the hook to fasten off. Follow the instructions for folded disk ears in A Variety of Ears on page 86 to prepare the ear for attachment later.

CROCHETING THE HEAD

Setup: Using the gray yarn, ch 2, 6 sc in 2nd ch from hook.

Rnd 1: 2 sc in each st around. Pull tail tight to close hole. (12 sc)

Rnd 2: *Sc in next st, 2 sc in next st; repeat from * around. (18 sc)

Rnd 3: *Sc in next 2 sts, 2 sc in next st; repeat from * around. (24 sc)

Rnd 4: *Sc in next 3 sts, 2 sc in next st; repeat from * around. (30 sc)

Rnd 5: *Sc in next 4 sts, 2 sc in next st; repeat from * around. (36 sc)

Rnd 6: *Sc in next 5 sts, 2 sc in next st; repeat from * around. (42 sc)

Rnd 7: *Sc in next 6 sts, 2 sc in next st; repeat from * around. (48 sc)

Attaching the Nose Roundies

Position the nose roundies in the center of the nose as shown below right. Thread a yarn needle with matching yarn, and whipstich all the way around the roundies to attach securely. Draw the yarn through the last stitch to fasten off, and weave in the tail on the wrong side.

Rnds 8–12: Sc in each st around. (48 sc)

Rnd 13: *Sc in next 6 sts, sc2tog; repeat from * around. (42 sc)

Rnd 14: Sc in each st around. (42 sc)

Rnd 15: *Sc in next 5 sts, sc2tog; repeat from * around. (36 sc)

Rnd 16: Sc in each st around. (36 sc)

Rnd 17: *Sc in next 4 sts, sc2tog; repeat from * around. (30 sc)

Rnd 18: Sc in each st around. (30 sc)

Rnd 19: *Sc in next 4 sts, 2 sc in next st; repeat from * around. (36 sc)

Rnd 20: *Sc in next 5 sts, 2 sc in next st; repeat from * around. (42 sc)

Rnd 21: *Sc in next 6 sts, 2 sc in next st; repeat from * around. (48 sc)

Rnds 22–24: Sc in each st around. Stuff partway with fiberfill. (48 sc)

Attaching the Eyes and Eye Roundies

Position the eyes and eye roundies as shown on the next page, and follow the instructions under Creating Faces on pages 84–85 to attach them securely.

Rnd 25: *Sc in next 6 sts, sc2tog; repeat from * around. (42 sc)

Rnd 26: *Sc in next 5 sts, sc2tog; repeat from * around. (36 sc)

Rnd 27: *Sc in next 4 sts, sc2tog; repeat from * around. (30 sc)

Stuff with fiberfill almost to the top.

Rnd 28: *Sc in next 3 sts, sc2tog; repeat from * around. (24 sc)

Rnd 29: *Sc in next 2 sts, sc2tog; repeat from * around. (18 sc)

Stuff completely with fiberfill. Pop in your precut, predrilled dowel with the screw hole facing out (see pages 88–89). Add more stuffing around the dowel, if necessary, to hold it firmly in place.

Rnd 30: *Sc in next st, sc2tog; repeat from * around. (12 sc)

Rnd 31: *Sc, skip the next sc; repeat from * around. (6 sc)

Slipstitch in first stitch of round, cut yarn, leaving a 6"-long tail, draw the tail through the loop on the hook to fasten off, and weave it in on the wrong side.

Attaching the Ears

Position the hippo's ears so that their sides are parallel with the sides of the head and the open edges are toward the front; see photo above. Use whipstitches to attach them securely, and draw yarn through the last stitch to fasten off. Weave in any loose ends.

Attaching the Teeth

Position the hippo's teeth directly under the nose roundies on the bottom of the chin, as shown on the previous page. Use the leftover tail of yarn to whipstitch them securely in place.

MOUNTING

See Mounting Your Critter's Head, beginning on page 89, for instructions on how to complete your taxidermy head.

Renegade Rhino

Finished Measurements

- 4″ wide × $6\frac{1}{2}$″ deep × $5\frac{1}{2}$″ tall

Hook

- US F/5 (3.75 mm) crochet hook

Yarn

- Worsted weight; 1 skein each of lilac and white

Other Supplies

- Two 12 mm clear plastic animal safety eyes
- Split-ring stitch marker
- Yarn needle
- Fiberfill
- Precut, predrilled dowel: 2″ diameter × 1″ long (see page 91)
- Prepared 7″ square plaque (see page 90)

CROCHETING THE EYE ROUNDIES

(make 2)

Setup: Using the lilac yarn, ch 2, 6 sc in 2nd ch from hook. Don't pull tight; leave a small hole where you can later insert the eyes. (Place a split-ring stitch marker to mark beginning of each round in the pattern, and move this marker up as you work each round.)

Rnd 1: 2 sc in each st around. (12 sc)

Slipstitch in first stitch of round, cut yarn, leaving a 12"-long tail for later use, and draw the tail through the loop on the hook to fasten off.

CROCHETING THE NOSE ROUNDIES

(make 2)

Setup: Using the lilac yarn, ch 2, 6 sc in 2nd ch from hook.

Rnd 1: 2 sc in each st around. Pull tail tight to close hole. (12 sc)

Slipstitch in first stitch of round, cut yarn, leaving a 12"-long tail for later use, and draw the tail through the loop on the hook to fasten off.

CROCHETING THE EARS

(make 2)

Setup: Using the lilac yarn, ch 2, 6 sc in the 2nd chain from hook.

Rnd 1: 2 sc in each st around. Pull tail tight to close hole. (12 sc)

Rnd 2: *Sc in next st, 2 sc in next st; repeat from * around. (18 sc)

Rnd 3: *Sc in next 2 sts, 2 sc in next st; repeat from * around. (24 sc)

Rnd 4: *Sc in next 3 sts, 2 sc in next st; repeat from * around. (30 sc)

Closing the ear: Slipstitch in first stitch of round, cut yarn, leaving a 12"-long tail for later use, and draw the tail through the loop on the hook to fasten off. Follow the instructions for folded disk ears in A Variety of Ears on page 86 to prepare the ear for attachment later.

CROCHETING THE TUSKS

Large Tusk

Setup: Using the white yarn, ch 2, 6 sc in 2nd chain from hook.

Rnd 1: 2 sc in each st around. Pull tail tight to close hole. (12 sc)

Rnds 3–8: Sc in each st around. (12 sc)

Following the instructions for Changing the Yarn Color on page 82, switch to the lilac yarn.

Rnd 9: Sc in each st around. (12 sc)

Slipstitch in first stitch of round, cut yarn, leaving a 12"-long tail for later use, and draw the tail through the loop on the hook to fasten off.

Stuff firmly to the top with fiberfill.

Small Tusk

Setup: Using the white yarn, ch 2, 6 sc in 2nd chain from hook.

Rnd 1: 2 sc in each st around. Pull tail tight to close opening. (12 sc)

Rnds 2–4: Sc in each st around. (12 sc)

Switch to the lilac yarn.

Rnd 5: Sc in each st around. (12 sc)

Slipstitch in first stitch of round, cut yarn, leaving a 12"-long tail for later use, and draw the tail through the loop on the hook to fasten off. Stuff firmly with fiberfill.

CROCHETING THE HEAD

Setup: Using the lilac yarn, ch 2, 6 sc in 2nd chain from hook.

Rnd 1: 2 sc in each st around. Pull tail tight to close hole. (12 sc)

Rnd 2: *Sc in next st, 2 sc in next st; repeat from * around. (18 sc)

Rnd 3: *Sc in next 2 sts, 2 sc in next st; repeat from * around. (24 sc)

Rnd 4: *Sc in next 3 sts, 2 sc in next st; repeat from * around. (30 sc)

Rnd 5: *Sc in next 4 sts, 2 sc in next st; repeat from * around. (36 sc)

Rnd 6: *Sc in next 5 sts, 2 sc in next st; repeat from * around. (42 sc)

Rnd 7: *Sc in next 6 sts, 2 sc in next st; repeat from * around. (48 sc)

Attaching the Nose Roundies

Position the nose roundies directly in the center of the nose as shown below. Thread a yarn needle with matching yarn, and whipstich all the way around the roundies to attach securely. Draw the yarn through the last stitch to fasten off, and weave the tail in on the wrong side.

Rnds 8–12: Sc in each st around. (48 sc)

Rnd 13: *Sc in next 6 sts, sc2tog; repeat from * around. (42 sc)

Rnd 14: Sc in each st around. (42 sc)

Rnd 15: *Sc in next 5 sts, sc2tog; repeat from * around. (36 sc)

Rnd 16: Sc in each st around. (36 sc)

Rnd 17: *Sc in next 4 sts, sc2tog; repeat from * around. (30 sc)

Rnd 18: Sc in each st around. (30 sc)

Rnd 19: *Sc in next 4 sts, 2 sc in next st; repeat from * around. Partially stuff with fiberfill. (36 sc)

Rnd 20: *Sc in next 5 sts, 2 sc in next st; repeat from * around. (42 sc)

Rnd 21: *Sc in next 6 sts, 2 sc in next st; repeat from * around. (48 sc)

Rnds 22–24: Sc in each st around. (48 sc)

Attaching the Eyes and Eye Roundies

Position the eyes and eye roundies as shown on the previous page, and follow the instructions under Creating Faces on pages 84–85 to attach them securely.

Rnd 25: *Sc in next 6 sts, sc2tog; repeat from * around. (42 sc)

Rnd 26: *Sc in next 5 sts, sc2tog; repeat from * around. (36 sc)

Rnd 27: *Sc in next 4 sts, sc2tog; repeat from * around. (30 sc)

Stuff with fiberfill almost to the top.

Rnd 28: *Sc in next 3 sts, sc2tog; repeat from * around. (24 sc)

Rnd 29: *Sc in next 2 sts, sc2tog; repeat from * around. (18 sc)

Stuff completely with fiberfill. Pop in your precut, predrilled dowel with the screw hole facing out (see pages 88–89). Add more stuffing around the dowel, if necessary, to hold it firmly in place.

Rnd 30: *Sc in next st, sc2tog; repeat from * around. (12 sc)

Rnd 31: *Sc, skip the next sc; repeat from * around. (6 sc)

Slipstitch in first stitch of round, cut yarn, leaving a 6"-long tail, draw the tail through the loop on the hook to fasten off, and weave it in on the wrong side.

Attaching the Ears

Position the rhino's ears so that their sides are parallel with the sides of the head and the open edges face front; see photo on previous page. Use whipstitches to attach them securely, and draw yarn through the last stitch to fasten off. Weave in any loose ends.

Attaching the Tusks

Position the itty-bitty tusk right between the eyes where the face dips in. Use whipstitches to securely sew the tusk in place. Position the larger tusk on the bulbous part of the face, and whipstitch it securely in place. Weave in loose ends on the wrong side.

MOUNTING

See Mounting Your Critter's Head, beginning on page 89, for instructions on how to complete your taxidermy head.

Lazy Lion

Finished Measurements

- 7″ wide × 7″ long × 4¼″ deep

Hook

- US F/5 (3.75 mm) crochet hook (for head and ears)
- US D/3 (3.25 mm) crochet hook (for mane)

Yarn

- Worsted weight; 1 skein of gold 
- Super-bulky faux fur; 1 skein of dark brown

Other Supplies

- One 22 mm black plastic animal safety nose
- Two 18 mm clear plastic animal safety eyes
- Split-ring stitch marker
- Yarn needle
- Fiberfill
- Precut, predrilled dowel: 2″ diameter × 1″ long (see page 91)
- Prepared 7″ square plaque (see page 91)

CROCHETING THE EARS

(make 4)

Setup: Using the gold yarn, ch 2, 6 sc in 2nd chain from hook. (Place a split ring stitch marker to mark beginning of each round in the pattern, and move this marker up as you work each round.)

Rnd 1: Sc in each st around. Pull tail tight to close hole. (12 sc)

Rnd 2: *Sc in next st, 2 sc in next st; repeat from * around. (18 sc)

Rnd 3: *Sc in next 2 sts, 2 sc in next st; repeat from * around. (24 sc)

Slipstitch in first stitch of round, cut yarn, leaving a 12"-long tail on two of the ears for later use and a 6"-long tail on the other two ears. Draw tails through slip stitch to fasten off. Weave in short tails on the wrong side and leave the long tails.

Place an ear with a 12"-long tail against an ear with the tail woven in with wrong sides facing. Thread the tail through a yarn needle and use it to whipstitch around the entire edge of each pair of ears. (See instructions for two-piece flat disk ears in A Variety of Ears on page 86.) Draw the yarn through the last stitch to fasten off and leave the tail for later use.

CROCHETING THE NOSE AND HEAD

Setup: With the gold yarn, ch 2, 6 sc in 2nd chain from hook. Don't pull tail tight; leave a small hole where you can later insert the nose.

Rnd 1: 2 sc in each st around. (12 sc)

Rnd 2: *Sc in next st, 2 sc in next st; repeat from * around. (18 sc)

Rnds 3–6: 1 sc in each st around. (18 sc)

Attaching the Nose

Position the nose as shown below, and follow the instructions under Creating Faces on pages 84–85 to attach it securely.

Rnd 7: Sc in next 6 sts, sc2tog, sc in next 8 sts, sc2tog. (16 sc)

Rnd 8: Sc in each st around. (16 sc)

Stuff firmly to the top with fiberfill.

Rnd 9: 2 sc in each st around. (32 sc)

Rnd 10: *Sc in first 3 sts, 2 sc in next st; repeat from * around. (40 sc)

Rnd 11: *Sc in first 4 sts, 2 sc in next st; repeat from * around. (48 sc)

Rnd 12: *Sc in first 5 sts, 2 sc in next st; repeat from * around. (56 sc)

Rnd 13: Sc in each st around. (56 sc)

Rnd 14: *Sc in first 6 sts, 2 sc in next st; repeat from * around. (64 sc)

Rnd 15: Sc in each st around. (64 sc)

Attaching the Eyes

Position the eyes close together and high on the head as shown on the facing page, and follow the instructions under Creating Faces to attach them securely.

For the sleepy-eye effect, cut a 12"–16" length of gold yarn and thread it through a yarn needle. Starting at the wrong side, come up at the inside edge of one of the eyes, over the eye, and down to the wrong side. Repeat until you get the desired effect. (See Sleepy-Eye Technique on page 87 for more information.) Repeat for the second eye.

Rnd 16: *Sc in next 6 sts, sc2tog; repeat from * around. (56 sc)

Rnd 17: *Sc in next 5 sts, sc2tog; repeat from * around. (48 sc)

Rnd 18: Sc in each st around. (48 sc)

Rnd 19: *Sc in next 4 sts, sc2tog; repeat from * around. (40 sc)

Rnd 20: *Sc in next 3 sts, sc2tog; repeat from * around. (32 sc)

Rnd 21: *Sc in next 2 sts, sc2tog; repeat from * around. (21 sc)

Rnd 22: *Sc in next st, sc2tog; repeat from * around. (16 sc)

Stuff with fiberfill almost to the top. Pop in your precut, predrilled dowel with the screw eye facing out (see pages 88–89). Add more stuffing around the dowel, if necessary, to hold it firmly in place.

Rnd 23: *Sc in next st, skip next st; repeat from * around. (10 sc)

Slipstitch in first stitch of round, cut yarn, leaving a 6"-long tail. Draw the tail through the loop on the hook to fasten off, and weave it in on the wrong side.

Creating the Lion's Mane

Using the dark brown faux fur yarn, sc into each st around the lion's head, starting about 6 rounds back from the base of the muzzle. After you complete the full circle around the head for the mane, slipstitch into the last stitch to fasten off; weave in the tail. Use your fingers, the crochet hook, or a special brush to fluff the mane and make it fuller. It's okay if some of the "fur" comes loose — that happens. (For more information, see Here Comes the Fuzz, page 88.)

Attaching the Ears

Position the ears 1 round behind the mane and, for a nice, perky look, just above the eyes as shown. Thread a yarn needle with matching yarn, and use it to whipstitch the ears along the bottom edge to attach securely. Draw the yarn through the last stitch to fasten off and weave in tail on the wrong side.

MOUNTING

See Mounting Your Critter's Head, beginning on page 89, for instructions on how to complete your taxidermy head.

Voilà! Your Lazy Lion is now complete.

Zippy Zebra

Finished Measurements

- 6½″ wide × 7″ long × 6½″ deep

Hook

- US F/5 (3.75 mm) crochet hook

Yarn

- Worsted weight; 1 skein each of black and white 4

Other Supplies

- Two 18 mm blue plastic animal safety eyes
- Split-ring stitch marker
- Yarn needle
- Fiberfill
- Precut, predrilled dowel: 2″ diameter × 1″ long (see page 91)
- Prepared 7″ round plaque (see page 90)

CROCHETING THE EYE ROUNDIES

(make 2)

Setup: Using the black yarn, ch 2, 6 sc in 2nd chain from hook. Don't pull tail tight; leave a small hole where you can later insert the eyes. (Place a split-ring stitch marker to mark beginning of each round in the pattern, and move this marker up as you work each round.)

Rnd 1: 2 sc in each st around. (12 sc)

Slipstitch in first stitch of round, cut yarn, leaving a 12"-long tail for later use, and draw the tail through the loop on the hook to fasten off.

CROCHETING THE NOSE ROUNDIES

(make 2)

Setup: Using the black yarn, ch 2, 6 sc in 2nd chain from hook.

Rnd 1: 2 sc in each st around. Pull tail tight to close hole. (12 sc)

Slipstitch in first stitch of round, cut yarn, leaving a 12"-long tail for later use, and draw the tail through the loop on the hook to fasten off.

CROCHETING THE EARS

(make 2)

Setup: Using the black yarn, ch 2, 6 sc in 2nd chain from hook.

Rnd 1: 2 sc in each st around. Pull tail tight to close hole. (12 sc)

Rnd 2: *Sc in next st, 2 sc in next st; repeat from * around. (18 sc)

Rnd 3: *Sc in next 2 sts, 2 sc in next st; repeat from * around. (24 sc)

Rnd 4: *Sc in next 3 sts, 2 sc in next st; repeat from * around. (30 sc)

Rnd 5: *Sc in next 4 sts, 2 sc in next st; repeat from * around. (36 sc)

Closing the ear: Slipstitch in first stitch of round, cut yarn, leaving a 12"-long tail for later use, and draw the tail through the loop on the hook to fasten off. Follow the instructions for folded disk ears in A Variety of Ears on page 86 to prepare the ear for attachment later.

CROCHETING THE NOSE AND HEAD

Setup: Using the black yarn, ch 2, 6 sc in 2nd chain from hook.

Rnd 1: 2 sc in each st around. Pull tail tight to close hole. (12 sc)

Rnd 2: *Sc in next st, 2 sc in next st; repeat from * around. (18 sc)

Rnd 3: *Sc in next 2 sts, 2 sc in next st; repeat from * around. (24 sc)

Rnd 4: *Sc in next 3 sts, 2 sc in next st; repeat from * around. (30 sc)

Rnd 5: *Sc in next 4 sts, 2 sc in next st; repeat from * around. (36 sc)

Attaching the Nose Roundies

Position the nose roundies as shown on the facing page, thread a yarn needle with matching yarn, and use whipstitches to attach them securely to the head. Draw yarn through last stitch to fasten off and weave in tail on the wrong side.

Rnd 6: *Sc in next 4 sts, sc2tog; repeat from * around. (30 sc)

Rnd 7: *Sc in each st around. (30 sc)

Following the instructions for Changing the Yarn Color on page 82, switch to the white yarn. From here to the end, you will alternate between the white and black yarns every 2 rounds to create the zebra's stripes. *Note:* You don't need to cut the yarn in this case when you change colors; simply carry the nonworking yarn up on the wrong side as you work.

Rnds 8 and 9: Sc in each st around. (30 sc)

Rnds 10 and 11: Switch to black, and sc in each st around. (30 sc)

Rnd 12: Switch to white, and *sc in next 4 sts, sc2tog; repeat from * around. (24 sc)

Rnd 13: Sc in each st around. (24 sc)

Rnd 14: Switch to black and *sc in next 3 sts, sc2tog; repeat from * around. (20 sc)

Rnd 15: Sc in each st around. (20 sc)

Stuff with fiberfill almost to the top.

Rnd 16: Switch to white, and *sc in next sc, 2 sc in next sc; repeat from * around. (30 sc)

Rnd 17: *Sc in next 2 sts, 2 sc in next sc; repeat from * around. (40 sc)

Rnd 18: Switch to black, and *sc in next 3 sts, 2 sc in next sc; repeat from * around. (50 sc)

Rnd 19: *Sc in next 4 sts, 2 sc in next sc; repeat from * around. (60 sc)

Rnd 20: Switch to white, and *sc in next 5 sts, 2 sc in next sc; repeat from * around. (70 sc)

Rnd 21: *Sc in next 6 sts, 2 sc in next sc; repeat from * around. (80 sc)

Attaching the Eyes and Eye Roundies

Position the eyes and eye roundies as shown above, and follow the instructions under Creating Faces on pages 84–85 to attach them securely.

Rnd 22: Switch to black, and *sc in next 6 sts, sc2tog; repeat from * around. (70 sc)

Rnd 23: *Sc in next 5 sts, sc2tog; repeat from * around. (60 sc)

Rnds 24 and 25: Switch to white, and sc in each st around. (60 sc)

Rnd 26: Switch to black, and sc in each st around. (60 sc)

Rnd 27: *Sc in next 4 sts, sc2tog; repeat from * around. (50 sc)

Rnd 28: Switch to white, and *sc in next 3 sts, sc2tog; repeat from * around. (40 sc)

Rnd 29: *Sc in next 2 sts, sc2tog; repeat from * around. (30 sc)

Stuff with fiberfill almost to the top.

Rnd 30: Switch to black, and *sc in next st, sc2tog; repeat from * around. (20 sc)

Place your precut, predrilled dowel into the back of the head with the screw hole facing out (see pages 88–89). Add more stuffing around the dowel, if necessary, to hold it firmly in place.

Rnd 31: *Sc in next st, skip next st; repeat from * around. (6 sc)

Slipstitch in first stitch of round, cut yarn, leaving a 6"-long tail, draw the tail through the loop on the hook to fasten off, and weave it in on the wrong side.

Attaching the Ears

Position the ears right above the eyes on the top of the head facing front to back as shown on the facing page. Thread a yarn needle with matching yarn, and whipstitch the bottom edge of the ears to the head. Draw the yarn through the last stitch to fasten off and weave in ends on the wrong side.

Making the Mane

My favorite part! Cut five 6" lengths of both the white and black yarns. Holding a length of each color together and starting just above the zebra's eyes, insert your crochet hook through a stitch and draw a loop of the yarns through, then fasten off by drawing the tails through the loop (like making fringe on a scarf). Repeat in each available open hole from the front to the back of the head. (See photo above for how to do this.) Add more yarn, if desired. Trim mane so that it stands straight up like a little zebra Mohawk. Now that's one rockin' zebra!

MOUNTING

See Mounting Your Critter's Head, beginning on page 89, for instructions on how to complete your taxidermy head.

Colossal Squid

Finished Measurements
- 7″ wide × 15½″ long × 3½″ deep

Hook
- US F/5 (3.75 mm) crochet hook

Yarn
- Worsted weight; 1 skein of lime green (4)

Other Supplies
- Two 18 mm blue plastic animal safety eyes
- Split-ring stitch marker
- Yarn needle
- Fiberfill
- Precut, predrilled dowel: 2″ diameter × 1″ long (see page 91)
- Prepared 8½″ × 11″ scalloped plaque (see page 90)

Abbreviation
- **sc tbl** Single crochet through back loop only (see page 201)

CROCHETING THE EYE STALKS

(make 2)

Setup: Ch 2, 6 sc in 2nd chain from hook. Don't pull tail tight; leave a small hole where you can later insert the eyes. (Place a split-ring stitch marker to mark beginning of each round in the pattern, and move this marker up as you work each round.)

Rnd 1: 2 sc in each st around. (12 sc)

Rnd 2: Sc tbl in each st around. (12 sc)

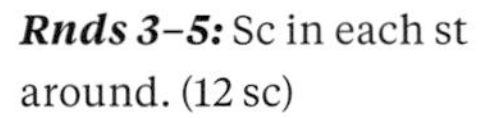

Rnds 3–5: Sc in each st around. (12 sc)

Slipstitch in first stitch of round, cut yarn, leaving a 12"-long tail for later use, and draw the tail through the loop on the hook to fasten off.

Attaching the Eyes

Pop in that big, blue plastic eye and secure the backing as described in Creating Faces on pages 84–85.

Stuff firmly to the top with fiberfill.

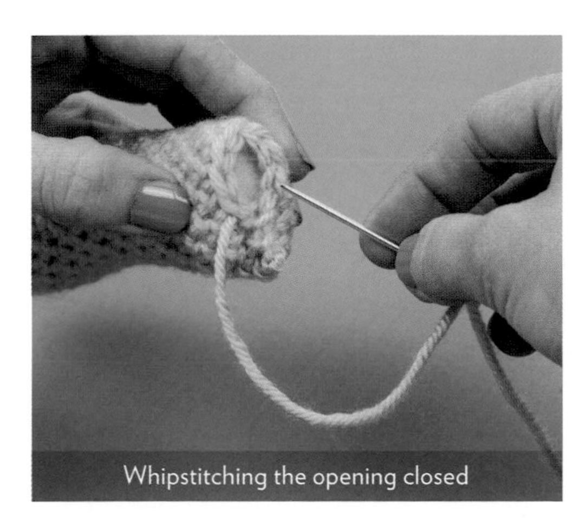

Whipstitching the opening closed

CROCHETING THE LONG TENTACLES

(make 2)

Setup: Ch 2, 6 sc in 2nd chain from hook.

Rnd 1: 2 sc in each st around. Pull tail tight to close hole. (12 sc)

Strap yourself in — this is the most time-consuming part of making your squid. Each long tentacle is a 9"-long, narrow tube.

Next Rnds: Sc in each st around until the piece is about 9" long, stuffing with fiberfill as you work.

Slipstitch in first stitch of round, cut yarn, leaving a 12"-long tail for later use, and draw the tail through the loop on the hook to fasten off.

Stuff the piece almost all the way to the top. Thread a yarn needle with matching yarn, pinch the top closed by folding it in half, and then whipstitch the opening closed. (See photo, bottom left, for how to do this.) Draw the yarn through the last stitch to fasten off and leave a tail for later use.

CROCHETING THE SHORT TENTACLES

(make 6)

The pattern for the short tentacles is essentially the same as for the long ones.

Setup: Ch 2, 6 sc in 2nd chain from hook.

Rnd 1: 2 sc in each st around. Pull tail tight to close hole. (12 sc)

Next Rnds: Sc in each st around until the piece is about 6" long, stuffing with fiberfill as you work.

Slipstitch in first stitch of round, cut yarn, leaving a 12"-long tail for later use, and draw the tail through the loop on the hook to fasten off.

Whipstitching two tentacles together

Place the two long tentacles together at their tops, and use matching thread to whipstitch them together (see photo above). Draw yarn through last stitch.

CROCHETING THE BODY

Setup: Ch 2, 6 sc in 2nd chain from hook.

Rnd 1: 2 sc in each st around. Pull tail tight to close hole. (12 sc)

Rnd 2: *Sc in next st, 2 sc in next st; repeat from * around. (18 sc)

Rnd 3: *Sc in next 2 sts, 2 sc in next st; repeat from * around. (24 sc)

Rnds 4–6: Sc in each st around. (24 sc)

Rnd 7: *Sc in next 3 sts, 2 sc in next st; repeat from * around. (30 sc)

Rnd 8: *Sc in next 4 sts, 2 sc in next st; repeat from * around. (36 sc)

Rnds 9–15: Sc in each st around. (36 sc)

Rnd 16 ("button-hole" for the dowel): Sc in next 19 sts, ch 2, skip 2 sts, sc in next 15 sts. See Making a Buttonhole on page 87. (36 sc, including the 2 ch sts)

Rnd 17: Sc in next 19 sts, 2 sc in ch-2 space, sc in next 15 sts. (36 sc)

Rnd 18: *Sc in next 4 sts, sc2tog; repeat from * around. (30 sc)

Rnd 19: *Sc in next 3 sts, sc2tog; repeat from * around. (24 sc)

Stuff with fiber-fill about halfway to the top. Insert the predrilled, precut dowel with the screw hole facing out (see pages 88–89). Add more stuffing around the dowel, if necessary, to secure it.

Rnds 20–29: Sc in each st around, stuffing with fiberfill as you work. (24 sc)

Rnd 30: Sc tbl in each st around. (24 sc)

Rnd 31: *Sc in next 2 sts, sc2tog; repeat from * around. (18 sc)

Rnd 32: *Sc in next st, sc2tog; repeat from * around. (12 sc)

Rnd 33: *Sc in next st, skip next st; repeat from * around. (8 sc)

Stuff firmly to the top with fiberfill.

Rnd 34: *Sc in next st, skip next st; repeat from * around. (4 sc)

Slipstitch in first stitch of round, cut yarn, leaving a 6"-long tail, draw the tail through the loop on the hook to fasten off, and weave it in on the wrong side.

ASSEMBLING THE PIECES

This is the fun part! Are you ready? Make sure the dowel is positioned so that the end of it is flush with the back of the squid.

The short tentacles form a ring around the long tentacles in the center.

Attaching the Eye Stalks

Place the body face up on a work surface and locate the spots for the eyes on opposite sides of the body just above those cool little loops you made by crocheting through the back loops in rnd 30. Thread a yarn needle with matching yarn and use whipstitches to attach the eyes stalks to the body. Draw the yarn through the last stitch to fasten off and weave in loose ends.

Attaching the Long Tentacles

Place the tentacles at the very bottom of the body as shown above. Thread a yarn needle with matching yarn and use whipstitches to sew on the tentacles. Draw the yarn through the last stitch to fasten off and weave in the tail.

Attaching the Short Tentacles

The loops that you created in rnd 30 are going to come in handy right about now. Using matching yarn, attach each of the six short tentacles to the squid's body by whipstitching through the loops and the stitches at the top of the tentacles. Fasten off and weave in the tail.

MOUNTING

See Mounting Your Critter's Head, beginning on page 89, for instructions on how to complete your taxidermy head. Note: Attach this head slightly above the center of the plaque. The ends of the tentacles will extend beyond the plaque.

Now, stand back and marvel at your squid's greatness. Congratulations! You have just completed one of the most involved patterns in the book.

Cute Cuttlefish

Finished Measurements

- 3½″ wide × 6″ long × 2″ deep

Hook

- US F/5 (3.75 mm) crochet hook

Yarn

- Worsted weight; 1 skein of yellow-green (4)

Other Supplies

- Two 18 mm blue plastic animal safety eyes
- Split-ring stitch marker
- Yarn needle
- Fiberfill
- Precut, predrilled dowel: 2″ diameter × 1″ long (see page 91)
- Prepared 5″ × 7″ oval plaque (see page 91)

Abbreviations

For illustrations of these stitches, see pages 200–201.

- **sc tbl** Single crochet through back loop only
- **hdc** half double crochet
- **dc** double crochet

CROCHETING THE TENTACLES

(make 6)

Setup: Chain 19. Leave a 12"-long tail for later use.

Rnd 1: Starting with 3rd chain from hook, hdc in next 8 ch, dc in next 8 ch. (16 sts)

Slipstitch in last chain, cut yarn, leaving a 12"-long tail for later use, and draw it through loop to fasten off.

CROCHETING THE BODY

Setup: Ch 2, 6 sc in 2nd chain from hook. (Place a split-ring stitch marker to mark beginning of each round in the pattern, and move this marker up as you work each round.)

Rnd 1: 2 sc in each st around. Pull tail tight to close hole. (12 sc)

Rnd 2: *Sc in next st, 2 sc in next st; repeat from * around. (18 sc)

Rnds 3–5: Sc in each st around. (18 sc)

You now can see your little cuttlefish head start to develop.

Rnd 6: *Sc in first next 2 sts, 2 sc in next st; repeat from * around. (24 sc)

Rnd 7: *Sc in each st around. (24 sc)

Rnd 8 ("buttonhole" for the dowel): Sc in next 12 sts, ch 2, skip 2 sts, sc in next 10 sts. See Making a Buttonhole on page 87. (24 sc, including the 2 ch sts)

Rnd 9: Sc in next 12 sts, 2 sc in ch-space, sc in next 10 sts.

Rnds 10–11: Sc in each st around. (24 sc)

Stuff the tip of the cuttlefish with a bit of fiberfill.

Rnd 12: *Sc in next 2 sts, sc2tog; repeat from * around. (18 sc)

Insert your precut and predrilled dowel into the buttonhole you created in rnd 8, making sure the screw hole faces out (see pages 88–89). Add more stuffing around the dowel, if necessary, to hold it firmly in place.

Stuff firmly to the top with fiberfill. Continue to add stuffing as you work.

Rnds 13–20: *Sc in each st around. (18 sc)

Attaching the Eyes

Locate the center front of your cuttlefish directly opposite the dowel on the back. Position the eyes on the sides at an equal distance from the center front as shown above, and follow the instructions under Creating Faces on pages 84–85 to attach them securely.

Stuff firmly to the top with fiberfill.

Rnd 21: *Sc tbl in next st, sc2tog; repeat from * around. (12 sc)

Continue stuffing with fiberfill.

Rnds 22 and 23: Sc2 tog around. (3 sc after rnd 23)

Slipstitch in first stitch of round, cut yarn, leaving a 6"-long tail, draw the tail through the loop on the hook to fasten off, and weave it in on the wrong side.

Attaching the Tentacles

Thread a yarn needle with the tail on one of the tentacles. Starting at the front of your cuttlefish, use whipstitches to sew the tentacle into those handy loops that you created in rnd 21. Attach the remaining tentacles in a circle around the bottom of the cuttlefish. They should all fit nicely in there. Weave in all loose ends. Voilà!

MOUNTING

See Mounting Your Critter's Head, beginning on page 89, for instructions on how to complete your taxidermy head. *Note:* Attach this head slightly above the center of the plaque. The ends of the tentacles will extend a bit beyond the bottom of the plaque.

Sleepy Octopus

Finished Measurements
- 6½" wide × 9" long × 4½" deep

Hook
- US F/5 (3.75 mm) crochet hook

Yarn
- Worsted weight; 1 skein of aqua

Other Supplies
- Two 18 mm clear plastic animal safety eyes
- Split-ring stitch marker
- Yarn needle
- Fiberfill
- Precut, predrilled dowel: 2" diameter × 1" long (see page 91)
- Prepared 9" × 7" oval plaque (see page 90)

Abbreviation
- **sc tbl** Single crochet through back loop only (see page 201)

Cut two 14"-long pieces of the aqua yarn and set them aside for later use when making sleepy eyes.

CROCHETING THE TENTACLES
(make 8)

Setup: Ch 2, 6 sc in 2nd chain from hook. (Place a split ring stitch marker to mark beginning of each round in the pattern, and move this marker up as you work each round.)

Rnd 1: 2 sc in each st around. Pull tail tight to close hole. (12 sc)

Rnds 2–20: Sc in each st around. (12 sc)

Stuff with fiberfill as you work.

Slipstitch in first stitch of round, cut

yarn, leaving a 12"-long tail, and draw it through the loop to fasten off. Stuff completely. Thread the tail through a yarn needle.

Pinch the opening closed by folding the tentacle in half (see page 187), and whipstitch shut. Draw the yarn through the last stitch to fasten off and leave the tail.

CROCHETING THE BODY

Setup: Ch 2, 6 sc in 2nd chain from hook.

Rnd 1: 2 sc in each st around. Pull tail tight to close hole. (12 sc)

Rnd 2: *Sc in next st, 2 sc in next st; repeat from * around. (18 sc)

Rnd 3: *Sc in next 2 sts, 2 sc in next st; repeat from * around. (24 sc)

Rnd 4: *Sc in next 3 sts, 2 sc in next st; repeat from * around. (30 sc)

Rnd 5: *Sc in next 4 sts, 2 sc in next st; repeat from * around. (36 sc)

Rnd 6: *Sc in next 5 sts, 2 sc in next st; repeat from * around. (42 sc)

Rnd 7: *Sc in next 6 sts, 2 sc in next st; repeat from * around. (48 sc)

Rnd 8: *Sc in next 7 sts, 2 sc in next st; repeat from * around. (54 sc)

Rnds 9–15: Sc in each st around. (54 sc)

Rnd 16 ("buttonhole" for the dowel): Ch 2, skip next 2 sts, sc in next 52 sts. Stuff with fiberfill. (54 sc)

Rnd 17: 2 sc in ch-2 sp, sc in next 52 sts.

Rnd 18: Sc in each st around. (54 sc)

Rnd 19: *Sc in next 7 sts, sc2tog; repeat from * around. (48 sc)

Rnd 20: Sc in each st around. (48 sc)

Attaching the Eyes

Place the octopus so that the opening you made in rnd 16 is down against the work surface. Position the eyes as shown below, and follow the instructions under Creating Faces on pages 84–85 to attach them securely.

Creating Sleepy Eyes

Thread a yarn needle with one of the two 14" pieces of yarn that you set aside when you began this project and use it to create the sleepy-eye effect on your octopus (see Sleepy-Eye Technique, page 87, for advice.) Fasten off the yarn on the wrong side and weave in the tail. Repeat with the other length of yarn for the second eye.

Rnd 21: *Sc in next 6 sts, sc2tog; repeat from * around. (42 sc)

Stuff with fiberfill almost to the top. Insert the precut, predrilled dowel into the hole at the back of the octopus with the screw hole facing out (see pages 88–89). Add more stuffing around the dowel, if necessary, to hold it firmly in place.

Rnd 22: Sc in each st around. (42 sc)

Rnd 23: *Sc in next 5 sts, sc2tog; repeat from * around. (36 sc)

Rnd 24: *Sc tbl in next 4 sts, sc2tog tbl; repeat from * around. (30 sc)

Rnd 25: *Sc in next 3 sts, sc2tog; repeat from * around. (24 sc)

Stuff with fiberfill as you work.

Rnd 26: *Sc in next 2 sts, sc2tog; repeat from * around. (18 sc)

Rnd 27: *Sc in next st, sc2tog; repeat from * around. (12 sc)

Rnds 28 and 29: *Sc in next st, skip next sc; repeat from * around. (4 sc after rnd 29)

Slipstitch in first stitch of round, cut yarn, leaving a 6"-long tail, draw the tail through the loop on the hook to fasten off, and weave it in on the wrong side.

Attaching the Tentacles

Thread a yarn needle with the tail you left on one of the tentacles, position it as shown above, and use whipstitches to attach it to the body. Fasten yarn off and weave in ends on the wrong side. Repeat to attach the remaining tentacles.

MOUNTING

See Mounting Your Critter's Head, beginning on page 89, for instructions on how to complete your taxidermy head. Voilà! You just completed your very own Sleepy Octopus.

Jiggly Jellyfish

Finished Measurements

- 3″ wide × 13″ long × 3″ deep

Hook

- US F/5 (3.75 mm) crochet hook

Yarn

- Worsted weight; 1 skein of turquoise (you can use either a light or bright turquoise) 4

Other Supplies

- Two 12 mm solid black plastic animal safety eyes
- Split-ring stitch marker
- Yarn needle
- Bright pink cotton embroidery floss
- Fiberfill
- Precut, predrilled dowel: 1¼″ diameter × 1″ long (see page 91)
- Prepared 5″ × 7″ plaque, with rounded corners (see page 90)

Abbreviation

For illustrations of these stitches, see pages 200–201.

- **sc tbl** Single crochet through back loop only
- **hdc** half double crochet

CROCHETING THE TENTACLES

(make 5)

Setup: Ch 48, turn.

Row 1: Hdc in 3rd chain from hook, then hdc in each ch to end of chain. (45 sc)

Slipstitch in last stitch, cut yarn, leaving a 12"-long tail for later use, and draw the tail through the loop on the hook to fasten off.

CROCHETING THE HEAD

Setup: Ch 2, 6 sc in 2nd chain from hook. (Place a split-ring stitch marker to mark beginning of each round in the pattern, and move this marker up as you work each round.)

Rnd 1: 2 sc in each st around. Pull tail tight to close hole. (12 sc)

Rnd 2: *Sc in next st, 2 sc in next st; repeat from * around. (18 sc)

Rnd 3: *Sc in next 2 sts, 2 sc in next st; repeat from * around. (24 sc)

Rnd 4: *Sc in next 3 sts, 2 sc in next st; repeat from * around. (30 sc)

Rnd 5: *Sc in next 4 sts, 2 sc in next st; repeat from * around. (36 sc)

Rnds 6 and 7: Sc in each st around. (36 sc)

Rnd 8 ("buttonhole" for the dowel): Ch 2, skip 2 sts, sc in the remaining 34 sts. (36 sc, including the 2 ch sts)

Rnd 9: 2 sc in ch-space, sc in the remaining 34 sts. (36 sc)

Rnd 10: *Sc in every st around. (36 sc)

Rnd 11: *Sc in next 4 sts, sc2tog; repeat from * around. (30 sc)

Attaching the Eyes

Hold your jellyfish so that the hole you made in rnd 8 is at the center back. Position the eyes as shown at right, and follow the instructions under Creating Faces on pages 84–85 to attach them securely.

Embroidering the Mouth

Thread a yarn needle with a length of embroidery floss, and starting on the wrong side, draw the floss through to stitch the little V-shaped mouth as shown.

Rnd 12: *Sc tbl next 3 sts, sc2tog; repeat from * around. (24 sc)

Stuff with fiberfill about halfway to the top.

Embroidering the mouth

Insert the precut, predrilled dowel into the hole you created in rnd 8, with the screw hole facing out and the end of the dowel flush with the back of the head (see pages 88–89). Add more stuffing around the dowel, if necessary, to hold it firmly in place.

Rnd 13: *Sc in next 2 sts, sc2tog; repeat from * around. (18 sc)

Rnd 14: *Sc in next st, sc2tog; repeat from * around. (12 sc)

Stuff firmly to the top with fiberfill.

Rnds 15 and 16: *Sc in next st, skip next st; repeat from * around. (4 sc after rnd 16)

Slipstitch in first stitch of round, cut yarn, leaving a 6"-long tail, draw the tail through the loop on the hook to fasten off, and weave it in on the wrong side.

CROCHETING THE WAVY SKIRT

Setup: Hold the jellyfish upside down and with its back facing you. Join matching yarn by slipstitching into one of the loops create in rnd 12.

Rnd 1: Working only in the loops created in rnd 12, * 5 hdc in next loop, skip next loop, slipstitch in next loop; repeat from * around (60 sts, including the slip stitches).

Slipstitch in first stitch of round, cut yarn, leaving a 6"-long tail, draw the tail through the loop on the hook to fasten off, and weave it in on the wrong side.

Attaching the Tentacles

Use the long tails on each tentacle to sew them to the bottom of the jellyfish's head right under the wavy skirt, as shown at right. Make sure to position them so they are evenly spaced. Fasten off each tail as you go and weave them in on the inside.

MOUNTING

See Mounting Your Critter's Head, beginning on page 89, for instructions on how to complete your taxidermy head.

APPENDIX

THE STITCHES AND ABBREVIATIONS

As a self-taught crocheter, it took me a long time to figure out what stitches and crochet techniques worked best for certain patterns and projects. Over the years, I have refined my skills and continue to learn and pick up new techniques along the way. The stitches described here include the basics, along with other stitches that I use everyday in my own projects and that are just useful to know. If you're a beginner, take your time to really get comfortable with these stitches. If you're a seasoned vet, feel free to dive right into your project and refer to the appendix when needed. Just remember to have fun!

FOUNDATION CHAIN OR CHAIN (CH)

Start by making a slip knot on your hook, then wrap the yarn over the hook (A) and pull a loop of yarn through the slip knot (B). That's 1 chain stitch.

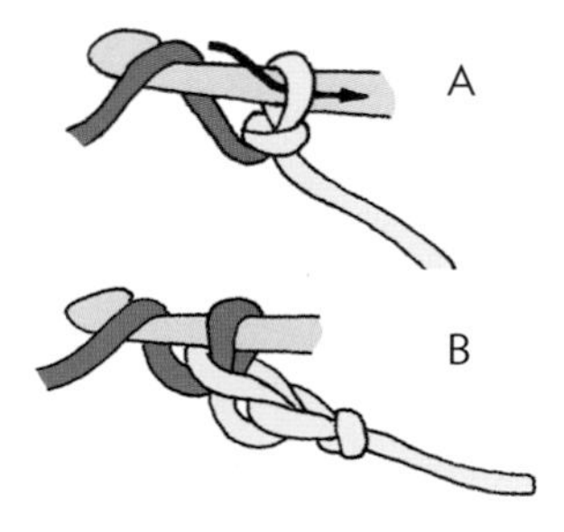

YARNOVER (YO)

Wrap the yarn over your crochet hook by bringing the yarn from behind the hook and wrapping it over the hook. (See drawing A for crocheting a chain, below left.)

SINGLE CROCHET (SC)

These drawings show how to single crochet into a chain. Insert the hook into the next stitch (or the stitch that's indicated), yarnover (A), pull a loop of yarn through (B), yarnover (C), and pull a loop through both loops on your hook (D). That's 1 single-crochet stitch.

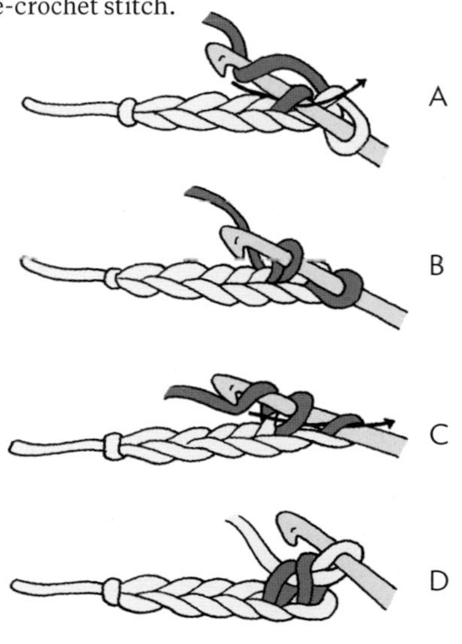

(continued on next page)

To single crochet into an established row, insert the hook under both top loops of the stitch in the preceding row, and then follow the same steps as before.

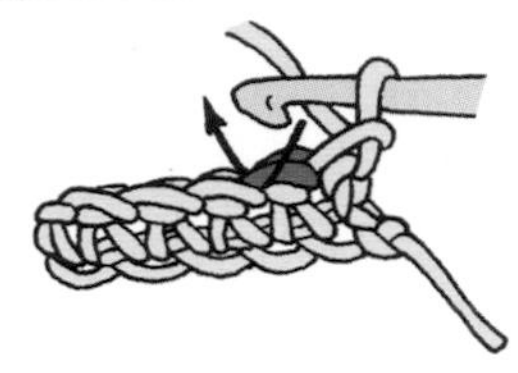

HALF DOUBLE CROCHET (HDC)

Yarnover and insert the hook into the next stitch (or the stitch that's indicated) (A), yarnover and pull a loop through (B). You now have 3 loops on your hook. Yarnover once more (C) and pull a loop through all 3 loops on the hook (D).

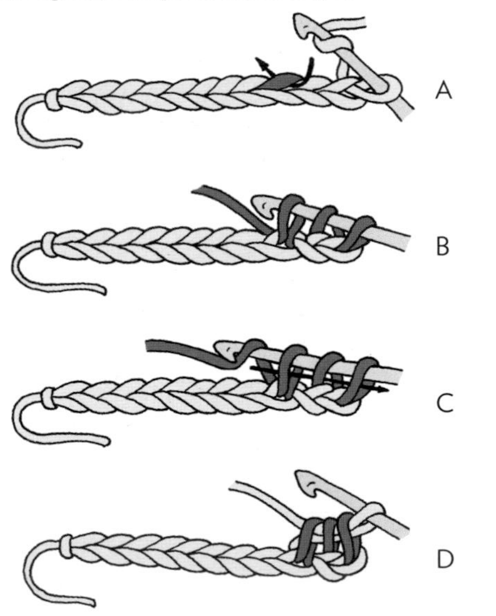

DOUBLE CROCHET (DC)

Yarnover and insert the hook into the next stitch (or the stitch that's indicated) (A), yarnover and pull a loop through. You now have 3 loops on your hook (B). Yarnover and pull a loop through the first 2 loops on your hook (C). You now have 2 loops on your hook (D). Yarnover (E), and pull a loop through the remaining 2 loops (F).

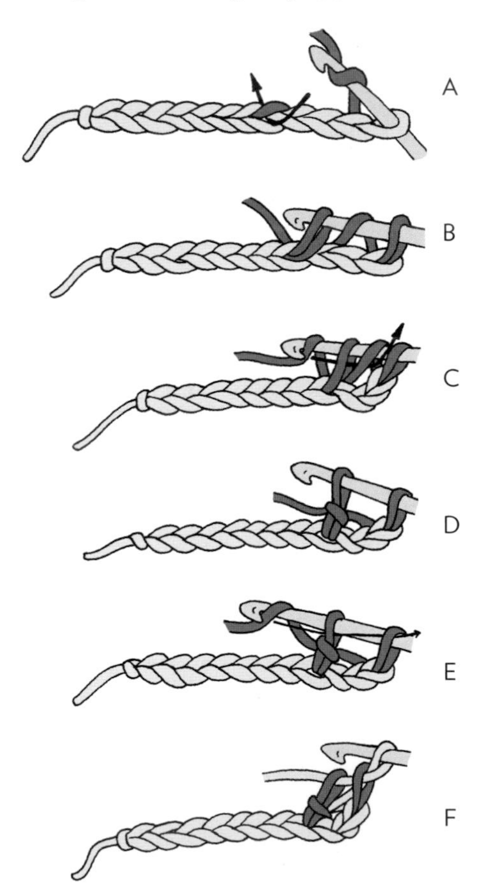

SINGLE CROCHET THROUGH BACK LOOP ONLY (SC TBL)

In most all of my patterns I work in both loops, but I sometimes specify to work in back loops only. I use this technique when I need to create an edge or a ridge to sew appendages to. To work a single crochet through back loop only (sc tbl), insert your hook into the back loop of the next stitch, yarnover, pull a loop of yarn through, yarnover, and pull a loop through both loops on your hook.

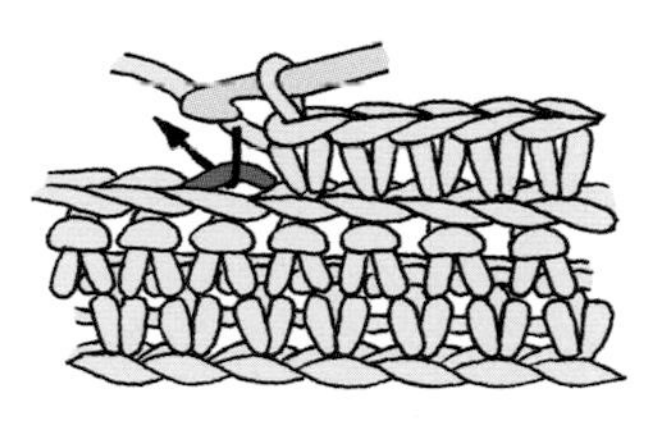

SINGLE CROCHET THROUGH FRONT LOOP ONLY (SC TFL)

In addition to working through only the back loop, I sometimes work through only the front loop. To accomplish this stitch, follow the directions above for sc tbl, inserting your hook through the front loop as shown in the illustration below.

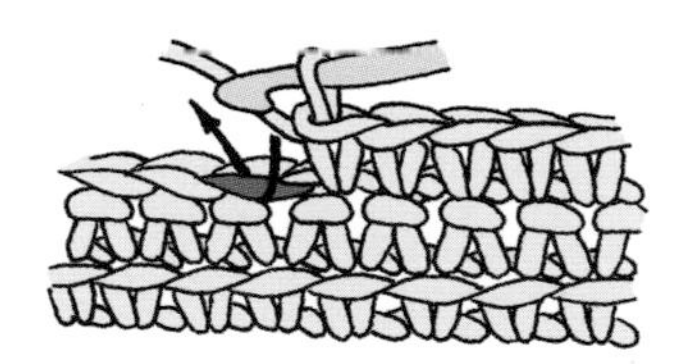

TURNING CHAIN

A turning chain is used to help transition from one row to the next. When you come to the end of one row, turn, chain 1 (or whatever number is indicated), and work back along the row. Note that the pattern will indicate more chains in the turning chain, depending on the height of the stitch that follows. In this book, the turning chain is counted in the total stitch count for a row, but that is not always the case.

SLIPSTITCH

With your last stitch on your hook, insert your hook through the space or chain where you want to place a slip stitch, yarnover, and pull a loop through the stitch and the loop on your hook with no further yarnover.

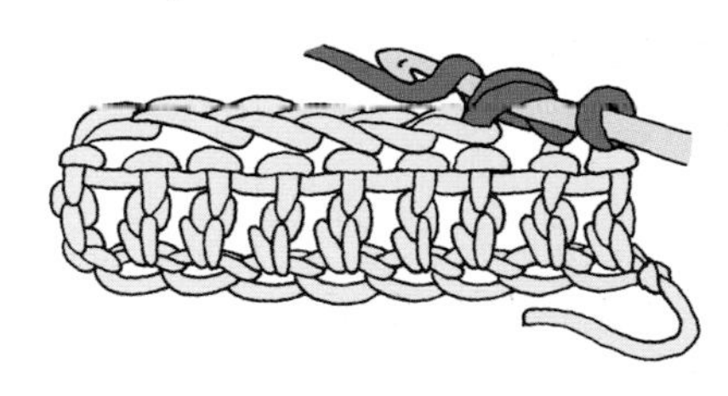

SINGLE CROCHET INCREASE

Work 2 single crochets into 1 single crochet.

SINGLE CROCHET DECREASE (SC2TOG)

This decrease is sometimes called single crochet 2 together. Insert your hook into the next stitch and pull a loop of yarn through. You will have 2 loops on your hook. Insert your hook into the next single crochet and pull through another loop of yarn. You will now have 3 loops on your hook (A).

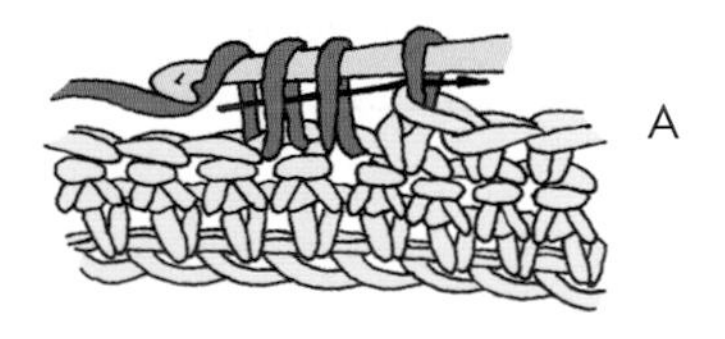

Yarnover and pull the yarn through all 3 loops on your hook (B). That, my friend, is a single crochet decrease.

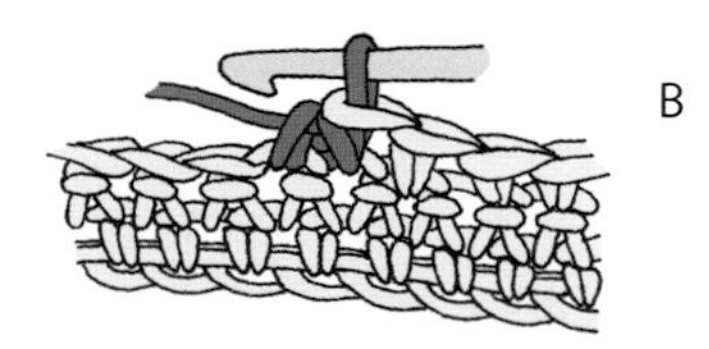

SUPPLIES AND MATERIALS

I've compiled a list of the materials that I think you'll find useful. It's always good to support your local shops, but some items aren't readily available in brick-and-mortar stores, so you may sometimes need to go online and order what you need. Some of the listed items are optional, so don't feel like you need to spend money on things you don't really need. I've been doing this for a while, so my kitty has grown substantially over the years of making these taxidermy critters.

GENERAL SUPPLIES

- Polyester fiberfill
- Yarn needles, size 18/22 or 20
- Embroidery scissors, small and sharp
- Split-ring stitch markers

CROCHET HOOKS

I use an F/5 (3.75 mm) crochet hook for most of the heads when I'm working with worsted-weight yarns. For some of the trims that are worked with specialty yarns, I use different sizes. The important thing is to be sure that you choose a hook size that will create a fabric dense enough to completely cover the fiberfill.

- F/5 (3.75 mm)
- E/4 (3.5 mm)
- D/3 (3.25 mm)

MOUNTING SUPPLIES

- **Dowel rods:** 1¼″ and 2″ diameters (project instructions specify size)
- **Pine board (for the moose):** 1″ × 6″ board, cut to 5″ round (about the size of a coffee-can lid or a CD)
- **Hacksaw or coping saw**
- **Screws:** Grip-Rite, Phillips head, fine thread, all purpose drywall screws, size 1⅝″ (4.128 cm)
- **Hand drill:** Phillips head 7/64 wood drill with a countersink bit (cordless, if available)
- **Fine-grain sandpaper,** for smoothing rough edges on plaques
- **Stain:** I use Minwax's English Chestnut 233
- **Craft foam brushes**, for staining plaques
- **Tape measure**
- **Hammer**
- **Picture hangers:** small nailess, adjustable, sawtooth
- **Plaque:** size as listed in each project supply list

OPTIONAL, BUT USEFUL, MOUNTING SUPPLIES

- **Drop cloth,** for use when staining
- **Plastic gloves,** for use when staining
- **Jigsaw or table saw,** for cutting dowel rods
- **Vise or clamp,** for support when cutting and predrilling the dowel rods
- **Scrap piece of wood,** for support when pre-drilling the dowel rods and test-staining the wood
- **Cloth towel or old cotton T-shirt,** to wipe after sanding
- **Smock**

METRIC CONVERSION

When the measurement given is **INCHES**
To convert it to **CENTIMETERS**
Multiply it by **2.54**

ACKNOWLEDGMENTS

First, I'd like to thank all my friends and family who have supported me throughout this journey. I'd also like to give a very special thanks to Martha Hopkins for her constant words of encouragement and guidance throughout the book-making process. Thank you to Deborah Balmuth and Gwen Steege for welcoming me into Storey with open arms. And to everyone at Storey who has helped make this book possible.

INDEX

Page numbers in *italic* indicate illustrations or photos.

Hook Yourself into the World of Crochet with More Storey Books

Crochet your way through the holidays with this collection of 18 fresh projects for stockings, ornaments, a tree skirt, garland, and more. Technique tutorials and pattern charts help take the stress out of holiday decorating.

EDIE ECKMAN

All the information crocheters need to unsnarl any project is in this essential reference. The accessible question-and-answer format has been revised and expanded and now includes detailed illustrations for both right-handed and left-handed crocheters.

EDIE ECKMAN

Turn your orphan skeins into charming treasures with these 101 designs for bags, scarves, gloves, toys, hats, and more. Crocheters of every skill level will find the perfect gift or personal indulgence to stitch with a single skein of yarn.

Edited by JUDITH DURANT & EDIE ECKMAN

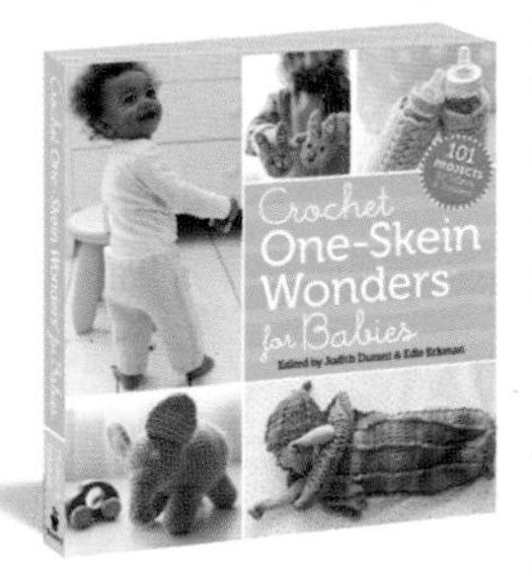

Show the little ones in your life lots of love with crocheted gifts. Each of these 101 adorable projects — including blankets, bootees, and beanies — use just one skein of yarn, so you can crochet a keepsake for your beloved bundle today.

Edited by JUDITH DURANT & EDIE ECKMAN

These and other books from Storey Publishing are available wherever quality books are sold or by calling 1-800-441-5700. Visit us at *www.storey.com* or sign up for our newsletter at *www.storey.com/signup*.